PHILIP'S

FAMILY
WORLD
ATLAS

PHILIP'S

FAMILY
WORLD
ATLAS

Published in Great Britain in 1997
by George Philip Limited,
an imprint of Reed Books,
Michelin House, 81 Fulham Road,
London SW3 6RB, and Auckland and Melbourne

Copyright © 1997 George Philip Limited

Cartography by Philip's

ISBN 0–540–07253–2

A CIP catalogue record for this book is available from the British Library

All rights reserved. Apart from any fair dealing for the purpose of private study,
research, criticism or review, as permitted under the Copyright Designs and
Patents Act, 1988, no part of this publication may be reproduced, stored
in a retrieval system, or transmitted in any form or by any means, electronic,
electrical, chemical, mechanical, optical, photocopying, recording, or otherwise,
without prior written permission. All enquiries should be addressed to the Publisher.

Printed in Hong Kong

Contents

World Statistics: Countries

This alphabetical list includes all the countries and territories of the world. If a territory is not independent, then the country it is associated with is named. The area figures give the total area of land, inland water and ice.

The units for areas and populations are thousands. The population figures are 1995 estimates. The annual income is the Gross National Product per capita in US dollars. The figures are the latest available, usually 1995.

COUNTRY/TERRITORY	AREA km² 1,000s	AREA miles² 1,000s	POPULATION 1,000s	CAPITAL	ANNUAL INCOME US $
Afghanistan	652	252	19,509	Kabul	220
Albania	28.8	11.1	3,458	Tirana	340
Algeria	2,382	920	27,936	Algiers	1,650
American Samoa (US)	0.20	0.08	58	Pago Pago	2,600
Andorra	0.45	0.17	65	Andorra La Vella	14,000
Angola	1,247	481	10,844	Luanda	600
Anguilla (UK)	0.1	0.04	8	The Valley	6,800
Antigua & Barbuda	0.44	0.17	67	St John's	6,390
Argentina	2,767	1,068	34,663	Buenos Aires	7,290
Armenia	29.8	11.5	3,603	Yerevan	660
Aruba (Neths)	0.19	0.07	71	Oranjestad	17,500
Australia	7,687	2,968	18,107	Canberra	17,510
Australian Antarctic Territory (Aus.)	6,120	2,363	0	–	–
Austria	83.9	32.4	8,004	Vienna	23,120
Azerbaijan	86.6	33.4	7,559	Baku	730
Azores (Port.)	2.2	0.87	240	Ponta Delgada	4,500
Bahamas	13.9	5.4	277	Nassau	11,500
Bahrain	0.68	0.26	558	Manama	7,870
Bangladesh	144	56	118,342	Dhaka	220
Barbados	0.43	0.17	263	Bridgetown	6,240
Belarus	207.6	80.1	10,500	Minsk	2,930
Belgium	30.5	11.8	10,140	Brussels	21,210
Belize	23	8.9	216	Belmopan	2,440
Benin	113	43	5,381	Porto-Novo	420
Bermuda (UK)	0.05	0.02	64	Hamilton	27,000
Bhutan	47	18.1	1,639	Thimphu	170
Bolivia	1,099	424	7,900	La Paz/Sucre	770
Bosnia-Herzegovina	51	20	4,400	Sarajevo	2,500
Botswana	582	225	1,481	Gaborone	2,590
Brazil	8,512	3,286	161,416	Brasilia	3,020
Brunei	5.8	2.2	284	Bandar Seri Begawan	9,000
Bulgaria	111	43	8,771	Sofia	1,160
Burkina Faso	274	106	10,326	Ouagadougou	300
Burma (= Myanmar)	677	261	46,580	Rangoon	950
Burundi	27.8	10.7	6,412	Bujumbura	180
Cambodia	181	70	10,452	Phnom Penh	600
Cameroon	475	184	13,232	Yaoundé	770
Canada	9,976	3,852	29,972	Ottawa	20,670
Canary Is. (Spain)	7.3	2.8	1,700	Las Palmas/Santa Cruz	7,900
Cape Verde Is.	4	1.6	386	Praia	870
Cayman Is. (UK)	0.26	0.10	31	George Town	20,000
Central African Republic	623	241	3,294	Bangui	390
Chad	1,284	496	6,314	Ndjaména	200
Chatham Is. (NZ)	0.96	0.37	0.05	Waitangi	–
Chile	757	292	14,271	Santiago	3,070
China	9,597	3,705	1,226,944	Beijing	490
Christmas Is. (Aus.)	0.14	0.05	2	The Settlement	–
Cocos (Keeling) Is. (Aus.)	0.01	0.005	0.6	West Island	–
Colombia	1,139	440	34,948	Bogotá	1,400
Comoros	2.2	0.86	654	Moroni	520
Congo	342	132	2,593	Brazzaville	920
Cook Is. (NZ)	0.24	0.09	19	Avarua	900
Costa Rica	51.1	19.7	3,436	San José	2,160
Croatia	56.5	21.8	4,900	Zagreb	4,500
Cuba	111	43	11,050	Havana	1,250
Cyprus	9.3	3.6	742	Nicosia	10,380
Czech Republic	78.9	30.4	10,500	Prague	2,730
Denmark	43.1	16.6	5,229	Copenhagen	26,510
Djibouti	23.2	9	603	Djibouti	780
Dominica	0.75	0.29	89	Roseau	2,680
Dominican Republic	48.7	18.8	7,818	Santo Domingo	1,080

COUNTRY/TERRITORY	AREA km² 1,000s	AREA miles² 1,000s	POPULATION 1,000s	CAPITAL	ANNUAL INCOME US $
Ecuador	284	109	11,384	Quito	1,170
Egypt	1,001	387	64,100	Cairo	660
El Salvador	21	8.1	5,743	San Salvador	1,320
Equatorial Guinea	28.1	10.8	400	Malabo	360
Eritrea	94	36	3,850	Asmara	500
Estonia	44.7	17.3	1,531	Tallinn	3,040
Ethiopia	1,128	436	51,600	Addis Ababa	100
Falkland Is. (UK)	12.2	4.7	2	Stanley	–
Faroe Is. (Den.)	1.4	0.54	47	Tórshavn	23,660
Fiji	18.3	7.1	773	Suva	2,140
Finland	338	131	5,125	Helsinki	18,970
France	552	213	58,286	Paris	22,360
French Guiana (Fr.)	90	34.7	154	Cayenne	5,000
French Polynesia (Fr.)	4	1.5	217	Papeete	7,000
Gabon	268	103	1,316	Libreville	4,050
Gambia, The	11.3	4.4	1,144	Banjul	360
Georgia	69.7	26.9	5,448	Tbilisi	560
Germany	357	138	82,000	Berlin/Bonn	23,560
Ghana	239	92	17,462	Accra	430
Gibraltar (UK)	0.007	0.003	28	Gibraltar Town	5,000
Greece	132	51	10,510	Athens	7,390
Greenland (Den.)	2,176	840	59	Godthåb (Nuuk)	9,000
Grenada	0.34	0.13	96	St George's	2,410
Guadeloupe (Fr.)	1.7	0.66	443	Basse-Terre	9,000
Guam (US)	0.55	0.21	155	Agana	6,000
Guatemala	109	42	10,624	Guatemala City	1,110
Guinea	246	95	6,702	Conakry	510
Guinea-Bissau	36.1	13.9	1,073	Bissau	220
Guyana	215	83	832	Georgetown	350
Haiti	27.8	10.7	7,180	Port-au-Prince	800
Honduras	112	43	5,940	Tegucigalpa	580
Hong Kong (China)	1.1	0.40	6,000	–	17,860
Hungary	93	35.9	10,500	Budapest	3,330
Iceland	103	40	269	Reykjavik	23,620
India	3,288	1,269	942,989	New Delhi	290
Indonesia	1,905	735	198,644	Jakarta	730
Iran	1,648	636	68,885	Tehran	4,750
Iraq	438	169	20,184	Baghdad	2,000
Ireland	70.3	27.1	3,589	Dublin	12,580
Israel	27	10.3	5,696	Jerusalem	13,760
Italy	301	116	57,181	Rome	19,620
Ivory Coast	322	125	14,271	Yamoussoukro	630
Jamaica	11	4.2	2,700	Kingston	1,390
Japan	378	146	125,156	Tokyo	31,450
Jan Mayen Is. (Nor.)	0.38	0.15	0.06	–	–
Johnston Is. (US)	0.002	0.0009	1	–	–
Jordan	89.2	34.4	5,547	Amman	1,190
Kazakstan	2,717	1,049	17,099	Alma-Ata	1,540
Kenya	580	224	28,240	Nairobi	270
Kerguelen Is. (Fr.)	7.2	2.8	0.7	–	–
Kermadec Is. (NZ)	0.03	0.01	0.1	–	–
Kiribati	0.72	0.28	80	Tarawa	710
Korea, North	121	47	23,931	Pyŏngyang	1,100
Korea, South	99	38.2	45,088	Seoul	7,670
Kuwait	17.8	6.9	1,668	Kuwait City	23,350
Kyrgyzstan	198.5	76.6	4,738	Bishkek	830

COUNTRY/TERRITORY	AREA km² 1,000s	AREA miles² 1,000s	POPULATION 1,000s	CAPITAL	ANNUAL INCOME US $
Laos	237	91	4,906	Vientiane	290
Latvia	65	25	2,558	Riga	2,030
Lebanon	10.4	4	2,971	Beirut	1,750
Lesotho	30.4	11.7	2,064	Maseru	660
Liberia	111	43	3,092	Monrovia	800
Libya	1,760	679	5,410	Tripoli	6,500
Liechtenstein	0.16	0.06	31	Vaduz	33,510
Lithuania	65.2	25.2	3,735	Vilnius	1,310
Luxembourg	2.6	1	408	Luxembourg	35,850
Macau (Port.)	0.02	0.006	490	Macau	7,500
Macedonia	25.7	9.9	2,173	Skopje	730
Madagascar	587	227	15,206	Antananarivo	240
Madeira (Port.)	0.81	0.31	300	Funchal	4,500
Malawi	118	46	9,800	Lilongwe	220
Malaysia	330	127	20,174	Kuala Lumpur	3,160
Maldives	0.30	0.12	254	Malé	820
Mali	1,240	479	10,700	Bamako	300
Malta	0.32	0.12	370	Valletta	6,800
Marshall Is.	0.18	0.07	55	Dalap-Uliga-Darrit	1,500
Martinique (Fr.)	1.1	0.42	384	Fort-de-France	3,500
Mauritania	1,030	412	2,268	Nouakchott	510
Mauritius	2.0	0.72	1,112	Port Louis	2,980
Mayotte (Fr.)	0.37	0.14	101	Mamoundzou	1,430
Mexico	1,958	756	93,342	Mexico City	3,750
Micronesia, Fed. States of	0.70	0.27	125	Palikir	1,560
Midway Is. (US)	0.005	0.002	2	–	–
Moldova	33.7	13	4,434	Chişinău	1,180
Monaco	0.002	0.0001	32	Monaco	16,000
Mongolia	1,567	605	2,408	Ulan Bator	400
Montserrat (UK)	0.10	0.04	11	Plymouth	4,500
Morocco	447	172	26,857	Rabat	1,030
Mozambique	802	309	17,800	Maputo	80
Namibia	825	318	1,610	Windhoek	1,660
Nauru	0.02	0.008	12	Yaren District	10,000
Nepal	141	54	21,953	Katmandu	160
Netherlands	41.5	16	15,495	Amsterdam/The Hague	20,710
Neths Antilles (Neths)	0.99	0.38	202	Willemstad	9,700
New Caledonia (Fr.)	19	7.2	181	Nouméa	6,000
New Zealand	269	104	3,567	Wellington	12,900
Nicaragua	130	50	4,544	Managua	360
Niger	1,267	489	9,149	Niamey	270
Nigeria	924	357	88,515	Abuja	310
Niue (NZ)	0.26	0.10	2	Alofi	–
Norfolk Is. (Aus.)	0.03	0.01	2	Kingston	–
Northern Mariana Is. (US)	0.48	0.18	50	Saipan	11,500
Norway	324	125	4,361	Oslo	26,340
Oman	212	82	2,252	Muscat	5,600
Pakistan	796	307	143,595	Islamabad	430
Palau	0.46	0.18	18	Koror	2,260
Panama	77.1	29.8	2,629	Panama City	2,580
Papua New Guinea	463	179	4,292	Port Moresby	1,120
Paraguay	407	157	4,979	Asunción	1,500
Peru	1,285	496	23,588	Lima	1,490
Philippines	300	116	67,167	Manila	830
Pitcairn Is. (UK)	0.03	0.01	0.05	Adamstown	–
Poland	313	121	38,587	Warsaw	2,270
Portugal	92.4	35.7	10,600	Lisbon	7,890
Puerto Rico (US)	9	3.5	3,689	San Juan	7,020
Qatar	11	4.2	594	Doha	15,140
Réunion (Fr.)	2.5	0.97	655	Saint-Denis	3,900
Romania	238	92	22,863	Bucharest	1,120
Russia	17,075	6,592	148,385	Moscow	2,350
Rwanda	26.3	10.2	7,899	Kigali	200

COUNTRY/TERRITORY	AREA km² 1,000s	AREA miles² 1,000s	POPULATION 1,000s	CAPITAL	ANNUAL INCOME US $
St Helena (UK)	0.12	0.05	6	Jamestown	–
St Kitts & Nevis	0.36	0.14	45	Basseterre	4,470
St Lucia	0.62	0.24	147	Castries	3,040
St Pierre & Miquelon (Fr.)	0.24	0.09	6	Saint Pierre	–
St Vincent & Grenadines	0.39	0.15	111	Kingstown	1,730
San Marino	0.06	0.02	26	San Marino	20,000
São Tomé & Principe	0.96	0.37	133	São Tomé	330
Saudi Arabia	2,150	830	18,395	Riyadh	8,000
Senegal	197	76	8,308	Dakar	730
Seychelles	0.46	0.18	75	Victoria	6,370
Sierra Leone	71.7	27.7	4,467	Freetown	140
Singapore	0.62	0.24	2,990	Singapore	19,310
Slovak Republic	49	18.9	5,400	Bratislava	1,900
Slovenia	20.3	7.8	2,000	Ljubljana	6,310
Solomon Is.	28.9	11.2	378	Honiara	750
Somalia	638	246	9,180	Mogadishu	500
South Africa	1,220	471	44,000	C. Town/Pretoria/Bloem.	2,900
Spain	505	195	39,664	Madrid	13,650
Sri Lanka	65.6	25.3	18,359	Colombo	600
Sudan	2,506	967	29,980	Khartoum	750
Surinam	163	63	421	Paramaribo	1,210
Svalbard (Nor.)	62.9	24.3	4	Longyearbyen	–
Swaziland	17.4	6.7	849	Mbabane	1,050
Sweden	450	174	8,893	Stockholm	24,830
Switzerland	41.3	15.9	7,268	Bern	36,410
Syria	185	71	14,614	Damascus	5,700
Taiwan	36	13.9	21,100	Taipei	11,000
Tajikistan	143.1	55.2	6,102	Dushanbe	470
Tanzania	945	365	29,710	Dodoma	100
Thailand	513	198	58,432	Bangkok	2,040
Togo	56.8	21.9	4,140	Lomé	330
Tokelau (NZ)	0.01	0.005	2	Nukunonu	–
Tonga	0.75	0.29	107	Nuku'alofa	1,610
Trinidad & Tobago	5.1	2	1,295	Port of Spain	3,730
Tristan da Cunha (UK)	0.11	0.04	0.33	Edinburgh	–
Tunisia	164	63	8,906	Tunis	1,780
Turkey	779	301	61,303	Ankara	2,120
Turkmenistan	488.1	188.5	4,100	Ashkhabad	1,400
Turks & Caicos Is. (UK)	0.43	0.17	15	Cockburn Town	5,000
Tuvalu	0.03	0.01	10	Fongafale	600
Uganda	236	91	21,466	Kampala	190
Ukraine	603.7	233.1	52,027	Kiev	1,910
United Arab Emirates	83.6	32.3	2,800	Abu Dhabi	22,470
United Kingdom	243.3	94	58,306	London	17,970
United States of America	9,373	3,619	263,563	Washington, DC	24,750
Uruguay	177	68	3,186	Montevideo	3,910
Uzbekistan	447.4	172.7	22,833	Tashkent	960
Vanuatu	12.2	4.7	167	Port-Vila	1,230
Vatican City	0.0004	0.0002	1	–	–
Venezuela	912	352	21,810	Caracas	2,840
Vietnam	332	127	74,580	Hanoi	170
Virgin Is. (UK)	0.15	0.06	20	Road Town	–
Virgin Is. (US)	0.34	0.13	102	Charlotte Amalie	12,000
Wake Is.	0.008	0.003	0.30	–	–
Wallis & Futuna Is. (Fr.)	0.20	0.08	13	Mata-Utu	–
Western Sahara	266	103	220	El Aaiún	300
Western Samoa	2.8	1.1	169	Apia	980
Yemen	528	204	14,609	Sana	800
Yugoslavia	102.3	39.5	10,881	Belgrade	1,000
Zaïre (= Democratic Republic of Congo)	2,345	905	44,504	Kinshasa	500
Zambia	753	291	9,500	Lusaka	370
Zimbabwe	391	151	11,453	Harare	540

World Statistics: Cities

This list shows the principal cities with more than 500,000 inhabitants (for Brazil, China, India, Japan, Russia and the USA only cities with more than 1 million inhabitants are included). The figures are taken from the most recent census or estimate, and are the population of the metropolitan area, e.g. greater New York, Mexico or Paris. All the figures are in thousands. Local name forms have been used for the smaller cities (e.g. Kraków).

AFGHANISTAN
Kabul 1,424
ALGERIA
Algiers 1,722
Oran 664
ANGOLA
Luanda 2,250
Argentina
Buenos Aires 10,990
Córdoba 1,198
Rosario 1,096
Mendoza 775
La Plata 640
San Miguel de Tucumán 622
Mar del Plata 520
ARMENIA
Yerevan 1,226
AUSTRALIA
Sydney 3,713
Melbourne 3,189
Brisbane 1,422
Perth 1,221
Adelaide 1,071
AUSTRIA
Vienna 1,560
AZERBAIJAN
Baku 1,081
BANGLADESH
Dhaka 7,832
Chittagong 2,041
Khulna 877
Rajshahi 517
BELARUS
Minsk 1,658
Homyel 501
BELGIUM
Brussels 952
BENIN
Cotonou 537
BOLIVIA
La Paz 1,126
Santa Cruz 767
BOSNIA-HERZEGOVINA
Sarajevo 526
BRAZIL
São Paulo 16,417
Rio de Janeiro 9,888
Salvador 2,056
Belo Horizonte 2,049
Fortaleza 1,758
Brasília 1,596
Curitiba 1,290
Recife 1,290
Nova Iguaçu 1,286
Pôrto Alegre 1,263
Belém 1,246
Manaus 1,011
BULGARIA
Sofia 1,114
BURKINA FASO
Ouagadougou 634
BURMA (MYANMAR)
Rangoon 2,513
Mandalay 533
CAMBODIA
Phnom Penh 920
CAMEROON
Douala 884
Yaoundé 750
CANADA
Toronto 4,344
Montréal 3,337
Vancouver 1,831
Ottawa–Hull 1,023
Edmonton 885
Calgary 831
Québec 693
Winnipeg 678
Hamilton 643
CENTRAL AFRICAN REP.
Bangui 706
CHAD
Ndjaména 530
CHILE
Santiago 4,628
CHINA
Shanghai 15,082
Beijing 12,362
Tianjin 10,687
Hong Kong (SAR)[1] 6,205
Shenyang 4,050
Chongqing 3,870
Wuhan 3,870
Guangzhou 3,750
Harbin 3,120
Chengdu 2,760
Nanjing 2,490
Changchun 2,470
Xi'an 2,410
Dalian 2,400
Zibo 2,400
Qingdao 2,300
Jinan 2,150
Hangzhou 1,790
Taiyuan 1,720
Zhengzhou 1,690
Shijiazhuang 1,610
Changsha 1,510
Kunming 1,500
Nanchang 1,440
Fuzhou, Fujian 1,380
Lanzhou 1,340
Anshan 1,204
Fushun 1,202
Ürümqi 1,130
Hefei 1,110
Ningbo 1,100
Guiyang 1,080
Qiqihar 1,070
Tangshan 1,044
Jilin 1,037
Linhai 1,012
Macheng 1,010
COLOMBIA
Bogotá 5,026
Cali 1,719
Medellin 1,621
Barranquilla 1,064
Cartagena 746
CONGO
Brazzaville 938
Pointe-Noire 576
COSTA RICA
San José 1,186
CROATIA
Zagreb 931
CUBA
Havana 2,143
CZECH REPUBLIC
Prague 1,217
DENMARK
Copenhagen 1,353
DOMINICAN REP.
Santo Domingo 2,100
Santiago 690
ECUADOR
Guayaquil 1,508
Quito 1,101
EGYPT
Cairo 9,656
Alexandria 3,380
El Gîza 2,144
Shubra el Kheima 834
EL SALVADOR
San Salvador 1,522
ETHIOPIA
Addis Ababa 2,316
FINLAND
Helsinki 525
FRANCE
Paris 9,469
Lyon 1,262
Marseille 1,087
Lille 959
Bordeaux 696
Toulouse 650
Nice 516
GEORGIA
Tbilisi 1,279
GERMANY
Berlin 3,475
Hamburg 1,703
Munich 1,256
Cologne 693
Frankfurt 660
Essen 622
Dortmund 602
Stuttgart 594
Düsseldorf 575
Bremen 552
Duisburg 537
Hanover 525
GHANA
Accra 1,390
Kumasi 540
GREECE
Athens 3,097
GUATEMALA
Guatemala 2,000
GUINEA
Conakry 1,508
HAITI
Port-au-Prince 1,402
HONDURAS
Tegucigalpa 739
HUNGARY
Budapest 2,009
INDIA
Bombay (Mumbai) 15,093
Calcutta 11,673
Delhi 9,882
Madras (Chennai) 5,361
Hyderabad 4,280
Bangalore 4,087
Ahmadabad 3,298
Pune 2,485
Kanpur 2,111
Nagpur 1,661
Lucknow 1,642
Surat 1,517
Jaipur 1,514
Coimbatore 1,136
Vadodara 1,115
Indore 1,104
Patna 1,099
Madurai 1,094
Bhopal 1,064
Vishakha-patnam 1,052
Varanasi 1,026
Ludhiana 1,012
INDONESIA
Jakarta 11,500
Surabaya 2,421
Bandung 2,027
Medan 1,686
Palembang 1,084
Semarang 1,005
Ujung Pandang 913
Malang 650
Surakarta 504
IRAN
Tehran 6,750
Mashhad 1,964
Esfahan 1,221
Tabriz 1,166
Shiraz 1,043
Ahvaz 828
Qom 780
Bakhtaran 666
Karaj 588
IRAQ
Baghdad 3,841
Diyala 961
As Sulaymaniyah 952
Arbil 770
Al Mawsil 644
Kadhimain 521
IRELAND
Dublin 1,024
ISRAEL
Tel Aviv 1,880
Jerusalem 562
ITALY
Rome 2,688
Milan 1,334
Naples 1,062
Turin 946
Palermo 695
Genoa 660
IVORY COAST
Abidjan 2,500
JAMAICA
Kingston 644
JAPAN
Tokyo–Yokohama 26,836
Osaka 10,601
Nagoya 2,159
Sapporo 1,732
Kobe 1,509
Kyoto 1,452
Fukuoka 1,269
Kawasaki 1,200
Hiroshima 1,102
Kitakyushu 1,020
JORDAN
Amman 1,300
Az-Zarqã 609
KAZAKSTAN
Almaty 1,198
Qaraghandy 613
KENYA
Nairobi 2,000
Mombasa 600
KOREA, NORTH
Pyŏngyang 2,639
Hamhung 775
Chŏngjin 754
Chinnampo 691
Sinŭiju 500
KOREA, SOUTH
Seoul 11,641
Pusan 3,798
Taegu 2,229
Inchon 1,818
Kwangju 1,145
Taejŏn 1,062
Ulsan 683
Puch'on 668
Suwŏn 645
Sŏngnam 541
Chŏnju 517
KYRGYZSTAN
Bishkek 597
LATVIA
Riga 840
LEBANON
Beirut 1,500
Tripoli 500
LIBYA
Tripoli 960
Lithuania
Vilnius 576
MACEDONIA
Skopje 563
MADAGASCAR
Antananarivo 1,053
MALAYSIA
Kuala Lumpur 1,145
MALI
Bamako 746
MAURITANIA
Nouakchott 600
MEXICO
Mexico City 15,643
Guadalajara 2,847
Monterrey 2,522
Puebla 1,055
León 872
Ciudad Juárez 798
Tijuana 743
Culiacán Rosales 602
Mexicali 602
Acapulco de Juárez 592
Mérida 557
Chihuahua 530
San Luis Potosi 526
Aguascalientés 506
MOLDOVA
Chişinău 700
MONGOLIA
Ulan Bator 619
MOROCCO
Casablanca 2,943
Rabat-Salé 1,220
Marrakesh 602
Fès 564
MOZAMBIQUE
Maputo 2,000
NEPAL
Katmandu 535
NETHERLANDS
Amsterdam 1,100
Rotterdam 1,074
The Hague 695
Utrecht 546
NEW ZEALAND
Auckland 929
NICARAGUA
Managua 974
NIGERIA
Lagos 10,287
Ibadan 1,365
Ogbomosho 712
Kano 657
NORWAY
Oslo 714
PAKISTAN
Karachi 9,863
Lahore 5,085
Faisalabad 1,875
Peshawar 1,676
Gujranwala 1,663
Rawalpindi 1,290
Multan 1,257
Hyderabad 1,107
PARAGUAY
Asunción 945
PERU
Lima–Callao 6,601
Callao 638
Arequipa 620
Trujillo 509
PHILIPPINES
Manila 9,280
Quezon City 1,667
Davao 868
Cebu 641
Caloocan 629
POLAND
Warsaw 1,643
Lódz 834
Kraków 745
Wroclaw 642
Poznań 583
PORTUGAL
Lisbon 2,561
Oporto 1,174
ROMANIA
Bucharest 2,061
RUSSIA
Moscow 9,233
St Petersburg 4,883
Nizhniy Novgorod 1,425
Novosibirsk 1,418
Yekaterinburg 1,347
Samara 1,223
Omsk 1,161
Chelyabinsk 1,125
Kazan 1,092
Ufa 1,092
Perm 1,086
Rostov 1,023
Volgograd 1,000
SAUDI ARABIA
Riyadh 2,000
Jedda 1,400
Mecca 618
Medina 500
SENEGAL
Dakar 1,729
SIERRA LEONE
Freetown 505
SINGAPORE
Singapore 2,874
SOMALIA
Mogadishu 1,000
SOUTH AFRICA
Cape Town 1,912
East Rand 1,379
Johannesburg 1,196
Durban 1,137
Pretoria 1,080
West Rand 870
Port Elizabeth 853
Vanderbijlpark–Vereeniging 774
Soweto 597
Sasolburg 540
SPAIN
Madrid 3,041
Barcelona 1,631
Valencia 764
Sevilla 714
Zaragoza 607
Málaga 531
SRI LANKA
Colombo 1,863
SUDAN
Khartoum 561
Omdurman 526
SWEDEN
Stockholm 1,539
Göteburg 783
SWITZERLAND
Zürich 915
SYRIA
Damascus 2,230
Aleppo 1,640
Homs 644
TAIWAN
Taipei 2,653
Kaohsiung 1,405
Taichung 817
Tainan 700
Panchiao 544
TAJIKISTAN
Dushanbe 524
TANZANIA
Dar-es-Salaam 1,361
THAILAND
Bangkok 5,876
TOGO
Lomé 590
TUNISIA
Tunis 1,827
Turkey
Istanbul 7,490
Ankara 3,028
Izmir 2,333
Adana 1,472
Bursa 1,317
Konya 1,040
Gaziantep 930
Icel 908
Antalya 734
Diyarbakir 677
Kocaeli 661
Urfa 649
Kayseri 648
Manisa 641
Hatay 561
Samsun 557
Eskisehir 508
Balikesir 501
UGANDA
Kampala 773
UKRAINE
Kiev 2,643
Kharkiv 1,622
Dnipropetrovsk 1,190
Donetsk 1,121
Odesa 1,096
Zaporizhzhya 898
Lviv 807
Kryvyy Rih 729
Mariupol 523
Mykolayiv 515
Luhansk 505
UNITED KINGDOM
London 6,967
Birmingham 1,220
Manchester 981
Glasgow 720
Liverpool 664
Leeds 529
Newcastle 525
UNITED STATES
New York 16,329
Los Angeles 12,410
Chicago 7,561
Philadelphia 4,944
Washington, DC 4,360
Detroit 4,308
San Francisco 3,866
Houston 3,530
Boston 3,211
Atlanta 3,143
Dallas 2,795
Minneapolis–St Paul 2,618
San Diego 2,601
St Louis 2,519
Baltimore 2,434
Pittsburgh 2,406
Phoenix 2,330
Cleveland 2,221
Seattle 2,124
Tampa 2,107
Miami 2,008
Denver 1,715
Kansas City 1,617
Portland 1,605
Cincinnati 1,560
San Jose 1,529
Norfolk 1,497
Milwaukee 1,450
Indianapolis 1,424
Sacramento 1,419
Columbus 1,394
San Antonio 1,379
New Orleans 1,303
Charlotte 1,212
Buffalo 1,194
Hartford 1,156
Salt Lake City 1,128
URUGUAY
Montevideo 1,384
UZBEKISTAN
Tashkent 2,113
VENEZUELA
Caracas 2,784
Maracaibo 1,364
Valencia 1,032
Maracay 800
Barquisimeto 745
Ciudad Guayana 524
VIETNAM
Ho Chi Minh 3,924
Hanoi 3,056
Haiphong 1,448
YEMEN
Sana 972
YUGOSLAVIA
Belgrade 1,137
ZAIRE
Kinshasa 3,804
Lubumbashi 739
Mbuji-Mayi 613
Kolwezi 544
ZAMBIA
Lusaka 982
ZIMBABWE
Harare 1,189
Bulawayo 622

[1] SAR = Special Administrative Region of China

GENERAL REFERENCE

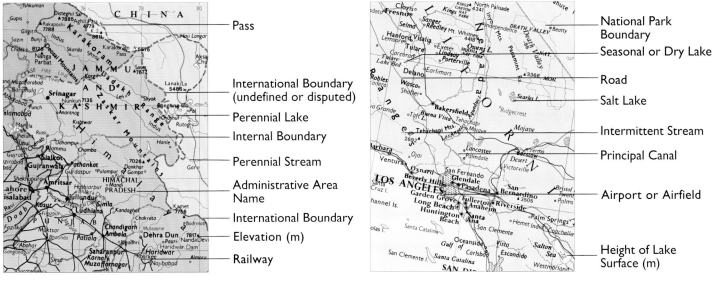

Pass

International Boundary
(undefined or disputed)

Perennial Lake

Internal Boundary

Perennial Stream

Administrative Area
Name

International Boundary

Elevation (m)

Railway

National Park
Boundary

Seasonal or Dry Lake

Road

Salt Lake

Intermittent Stream

Principal Canal

Airport or Airfield

Height of Lake
Surface (m)

Settlements

Settlement symbols and type styles vary according to the scale of each map and indicate the importance of towns rather than specific population figures.

TIME ZONES

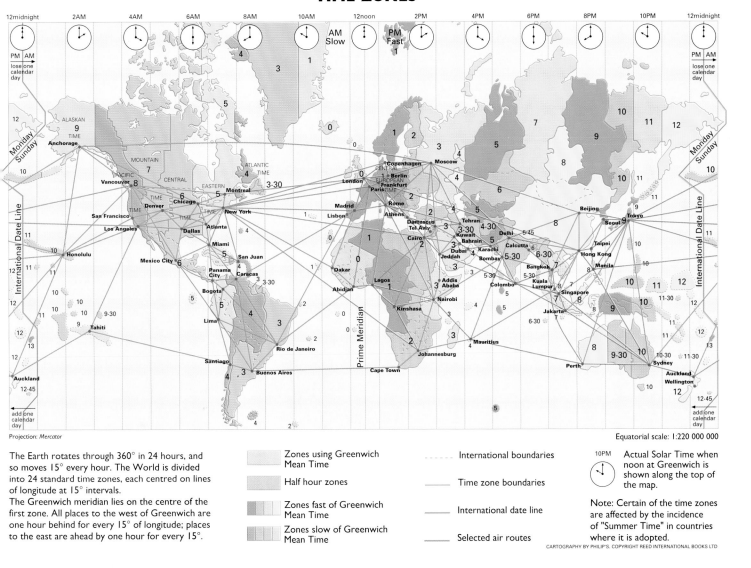

Projection: Mercator

Equatorial scale: 1:220 000 000

The Earth rotates through 360° in 24 hours, and so moves 15° every hour. The World is divided into 24 standard time zones, each centred on lines of longitude at 15° intervals.
The Greenwich meridian lies on the centre of the first zone. All places to the west of Greenwich are one hour behind for every 15° of longitude; places to the east are ahead by one hour for every 15°.

Zones using Greenwich Mean Time

Half hour zones

Zones fast of Greenwich Mean Time

Zones slow of Greenwich Mean Time

International boundaries

Time zone boundaries

International date line

Selected air routes

10PM Actual Solar Time when noon at Greenwich is shown along the top of the map.

Note: Certain of the time zones are affected by the incidence of "Summer Time" in countries where it is adopted.

CARTOGRAPHY BY PHILIP'S. COPYRIGHT REED INTERNATIONAL BOOKS LTD

1 2 3 4 5 6 7 8 9

A

Beaufort
Sea Banks I. Parry Is. Queen Elizabeth Is. Ellesmere I. GREENLAND
St. Lawrence I. Bering Strait Victoria I. Devon I. Baffin (Denmark) Arctic C
Yukon Fairbanks *Great Bear L.* Baffin I. *Baffin Bay* Denmark Str.
ALASKA Anchorage Yellowknife *Bay* Godthåb ICELAND
(U.S.A.) Great Slave L. *Hudson Davis Str.* Reykjavik Faroe Is.
B Aleutian Is.(U.S.A.) Kodiak I. Mackenzie *Bay* Scheffervile (Den.)
Queen C A N A D A UNITED
Charlotte Is. Edmonton Nelson Churchill KINGDOM
Vancouver Calgary Winnipeg L. Superior Newfoundland Glasgow
Vancouver I. Winnipeg Quebec St. John's Dublin
Seattle Missouri L. Huron Ottawa Montreal Halifax IRELAND LOND
Portland UNITED STATES Minneapolis Michigan Toronto Boston
Salt Lake Milwaukee Detroit Cleveland New York FR
City Denver CHICAGO Pittsburgh PHILADELPHIA PORTUGAL Bord
SAN FRANCISCO Sacramento Kansas City St. Louis Cincinnati Baltimore N O R T H Lisbon SP
C OF AMERICA Memphis Washington D.C. Azores
LOS ANGELES Phoenix Dallas Atlanta Bermuda (Port.) Tangier
San Diego El Paso Houston (U.K.) A T L A N T I C Rabat
Ciudad Juárez New Jacksonville Casablanca
Guadalupe I. Monterrey Orleans MOROCCO
(Mexico) Gulf of Miami Madeira Marrakesh
Tropic of Cancer MEXICO Mexico Havana BAHAMAS O C E A N (Port.) El Aaiun
Revilla León CUBA Canary Is. WESTERN
Gigedo Is. Guadalajara Turks & Caicos (Sp.) SAHARA
(Mexico) MÉXICO Cayman Is.(U.K.) (U.K.) CAPE VERDE Nouakchott MAURITANIA
Puebla Port-au-Prince HAITI DOMINICAN REP. IS. Timbukt
GUATEMALA Belmopan JAMAICA Santo Virgin Is. (U.S.A.)&(U.K.) Dakar SENEGAL
BELIZE Kingston Domingo PUERTO ANTIGUA & BARBUDA GAMBIA Bamako
D Guatemala HONDURAS RICO ST. KITTS - NEVIS GUINEA-BISSAU Ouagad
San Salvador Tegucigalpa *Caribbean* GUADELOUPE (Fr.) DOMINICA Bissau
EL SALVADOR NICARAGUA *Sea* MARTINIQUE (Fr.) ST. LUCIA Conakry IVOR
Managua NETH.- ST. VINCENT BARBADOS Freetown COAS
Clipperton I. Barranquilla ANTILLES THE GRENADINES GRENADA SIERRA LEONE
(Fr.) San José Panamá Caracas TRINIDAD & Monrovia LIBERIA
COSTA RICA PANAMÁ Orinoco TOBAGO Abidjan
Medellín VENEZUELA Georgetown Gulf
Cocos I. Cali GUYANA Paramaribo
(C.Rica) BOGOTÁ SURINAM Cayenne
Malpelo I. COLOMBIA FRENCH
(Colombia) GUIANA São Paulo
Galápagos Quito Negro (Brazil)
(Ecuador) ECUADOR Belém Fortaleza
Guayaquil Iquitos Manaus Amazon Fernando de Noronha
(Brazil)
Equator Japurá Natal Ascension I.
(U.K.)
B R A Z I L Recife
PERU Ucayali Madeira Tocantins
E LIMA Salvador
Callao São Francisco
L. Titicaca Brasília St. Helena
Arequipa La Paz (U.K.)
BOLIVIA Belo Horizonte S O U T H
Sucre
SÃO PAULO RIO DE JANEIRO Trindade
Antofagasta PARAGUAY Santos (Brazil)
Asunción Curitiba A T L A N T I C
Tucumán Pôrto Alegre
San Felix San Ambrosio Paraná Rio Grande
(Chile) (Chile) Córdoba Uruguay O C E A N
Valparaíso Rosario URUGUAY Tristan da Cu
Juan Fernández SANTIAGO Paraná Montevideo (U.K.)
F (Chile) Talcahuano BUENOS AIRES Gough I.
ARGENTINA (U.K.)
Bahía Blanca

Chiloé I.

Falkland Is.
(U.K.) South Georgia
Punta Arenas Tierra del Fuego (U.K.)
C. Horn *Scotia Sea* South Sandwich Is.
G (U.K.)
Drake Passage South Orkney Is.
South Shetland Is. (U.K.)
(U.K.)
Antarctic Circle *Bellingshausen Sea* *Weddell*
Sea
Amundsen Sea A n t a a
H West from Green

Hanoi ● Capital Cities

CARTOGRAPHY BY PHILIP'S. COPYRIGHT REED INTERNATIONAL BOOKS LTD.

1 : 20 000 000

100   0   100   200   300   400 miles

100   0   100   200   300   400   500   600 km

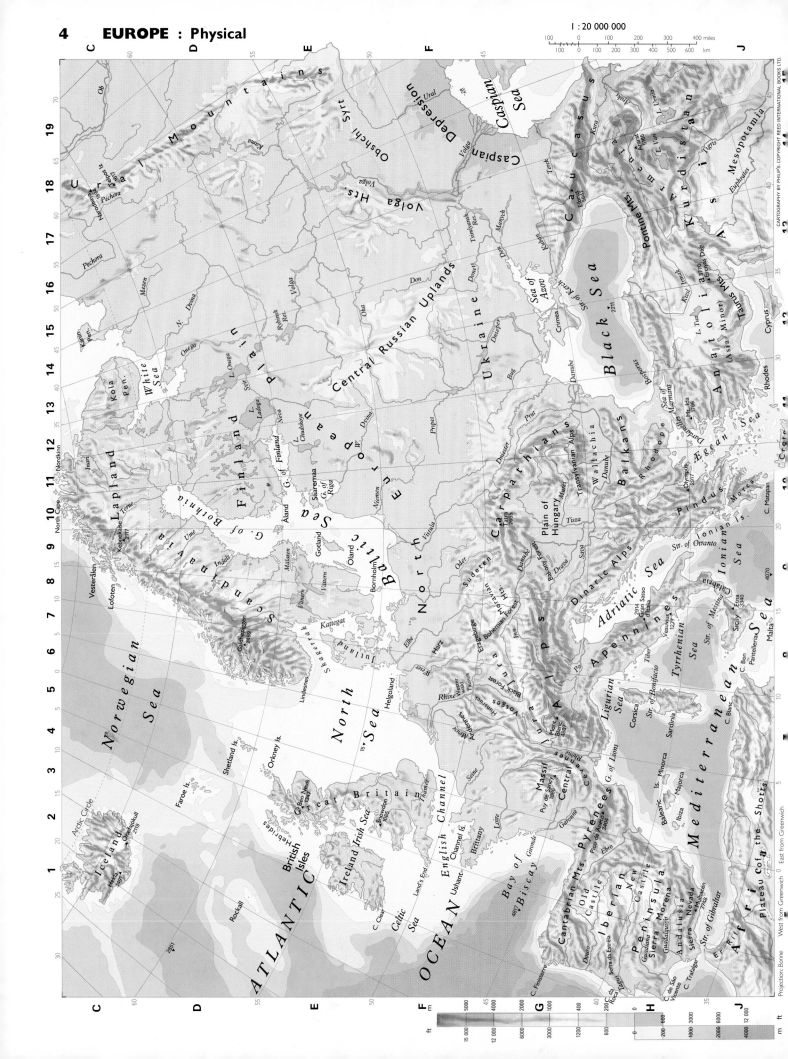

CARTOGRAPHY BY PHILIP'S. COPYRIGHT REED INTERNATIONAL BOOKS LTD.

Projection: Bonne

West from Greenwich   East from Greenwich

Cartographer: Borrie

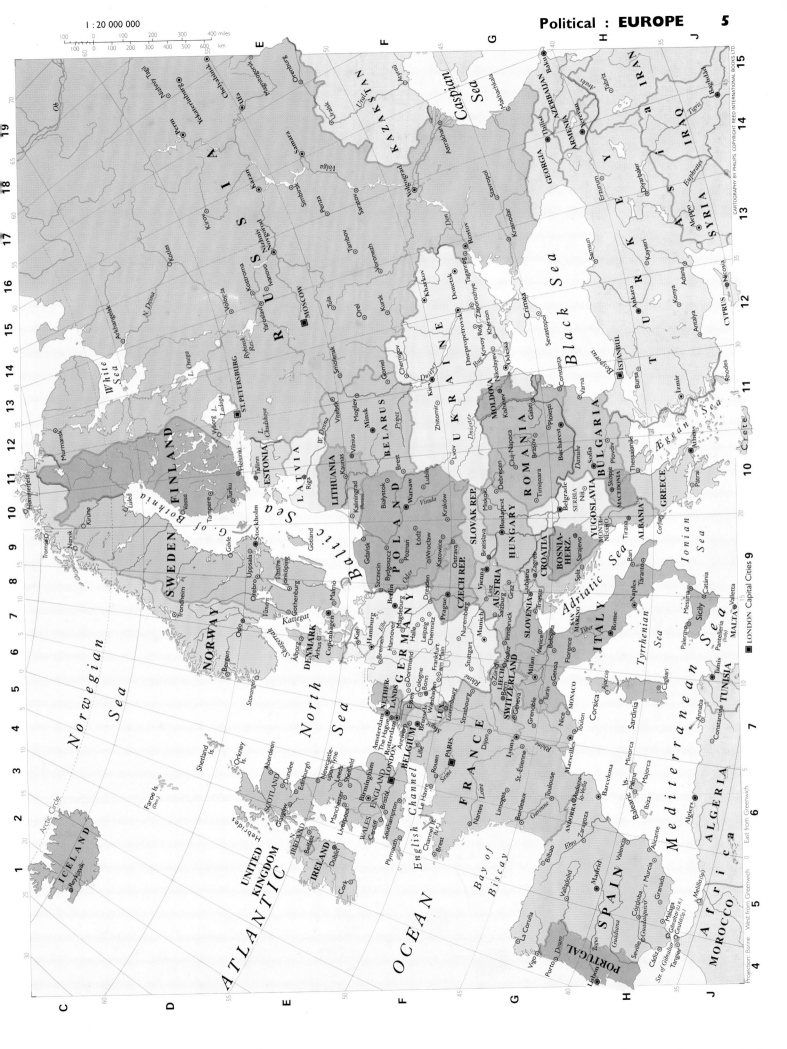

1:10 000 000

ICELAND
On the same scale   West from Greenwich

Projection: *Conical with two standard parallels*

COPYRIGHT. GEORGE PHILIP & SON. LTD.

East from Greenwich

1 : 5 000 000

50   0   50   100 miles
50   0   50   100   150 km

1   2   3   4   5   6   7   8   9

A T L A N T I C   O C E A N

1224

316

NORWAY

Askøy
Bergen
Osøyti
Stord
Bømlo
Leitvik
Haugesund
Kopervik
Åkrahamn
Boknafjorden
Stavanger
Sandnes
Bryne
Nærbø

Shetland Is.
Yell
Unst
Fetlar
Foula
Mainland
Lerwick

Fair Isle

Orkney Is.
Westray
Sanday
Stronsay
Mainland
Kirkwall
Hoy
South Ronaldsay

Pentland Firth
C. Wrath
Thurso
Wick
Helmsdale

N O R T H

S E A

238

Outer Hebrides
Lewis
Stornoway
St. Kilda
789
Harris
North Uist
Benbecula
South Uist
Inner Hebrides
Skye
Barra
Rhum
Eigg
Coll
Tobermory
Tiree
Mull
Colonsay
Mallaig
Fort William
Ben Nevis
1342
1214

North West Highlands
Ullapool
Lairg
Golspie
Tain
Invergordon
Dingwall
Nairn
Inverness
Aviemore
L. Ness
1182
Elgin
Buckie
Banff
Fraserburgh
Peterhead
Huntly
Inverurie
Moray Firth
Grampian Mts.
1311
Aberdeen
Stonehaven
Don
Dee
Ballater
SCOTLAND
Spey
Forfar
Montrose
Arbroath
Tay
Perth
Dundee
St. Andrews

Jura
Islay
Arran
Campbeltown
973
L. Lomond
Stirling
Greenock
Paisley
Glasgow
East Kilbride
Hamilton
Irvine
Kilmarnock
Ayr
Girvan
Dunfermline
Kirkcaldy
Glenrothes
Dunbar
Edinburgh
Southern Uplands
840
Galashiels
Jedburgh
Hawick
Berwick-upon-Tweed
Cheviot Hills
816
Alnwick

C E L T I C

S E A

North Channel
Malin Hd.
Aran I.
Buncrana
Letterkenny
Coleraine
Londonderry
Ballymena
Larne
Lifford
Donegal
Strabane
Omagh
Bangor
NORTHERN IRELAND
Ulster
Lough Neagh
Belfast
Bundoran
Lower L. Erne
Enniskillen
Clones
Armagh
Lurgan
Lisburn
Portadown
Newry
Mull of Galloway
Stranraer
Kirkcudbright
Workington
Whitehaven
Annan
Carlisle
Hexham
Dumfries
Firth of Clyde
Firth of Forth

Dingle
Tralee
Killarney
Mallow
Bandon
Kinsale
Cork
Cóbh
Youghal
Dungarvan
Waterford
Carrick-on-Suir
Clonmel
Tipperary
Thurles
Limerick
Ennis
Kilrush
Listowel
Macgillycuddy's Reeks
1041
Carrauntoohill
99
C. Clear
Bantry

Achill I.
Ballina
Castlebar
L. Conn
Westport
Connemara
Lough Mask
Galway B.
Galway
Aran Is.
Roscommon
L. Corrib
Ballinasloe
Athlone
Lough Ree
Birr
Tullamore
Mullingar
Longford
Leitrim
Cavan
Ceanannus Mor
Boyne
Drogheda
Sligo
Castleblaney
Dundalk
Monaghan
IRELAND
Nenagh
Carlow
Kilkenny
Athy
Port Laoise
926
Wicklow Mts.
Arklow
Dublin
Dun Laoghaire
Bray
Wexford
Rosslare

I R I S H

S E A

Douglas
I. of Man
Cumbrian Mts.
978
Barrow-in-Furness
Lancaster
893
Darlington
Durham
Hartlepool
Redcar
Middlesbrough
Stockton-on-Tees
Scarborough
Bridlington
Newcastle-upon-Tyne
South Shields
Sunderland
Gateshead
Pennines

UNITED
KINGDOM

ENGLAND

Holyhead
Anglesey
Bangor
Colwyn Bay
Llandudno
Conwy
Chester
Crewe
1085
Snowdon
Cambrian Mts.
Wrexham
Welshpool
Shrewsbury
Telford

Blackpool
Preston
Blackburn
Burnley
Keighley
Bradford
Halifax
Huddersfield
Bolton
Oldham
Manchester
Liverpool
Warrington
Stockport
636
Stoke on Trent
Sheffield
Chesterfield
Rotherham
Barnsley
Harrogate
Leeds
York
Beverley
Kingston upon Hull
Humber
Grimsby
Scunthorpe
Doncaster
Lincoln
Louth
Skegness
The Wash
Boston
Cromer

Pwllheli
Cardigan Bay
Aberystwyth
WALES
Carmarthen
Brecon
886
Merthyr Tydfil
Neath
Llanelli
Swansea
Port Talbot
Barry
Cardiff
Newport
Rhondda
Cwmbran
Bristol Channel

Derby
Nottingham
Trent
Mansfield
Grantham
Leicester
Nuneaton
BIRMINGHAM
Wolverhampton
Coventry
Rugby
Corby
Peterborough
King's Lynn
Norwich
Great Yarmouth
Lowestoft
Ely
Thetford
Bury St. Edmunds
Cambridge
Ipswich
Felixstowe
Harwich
Colchester
Chelmsford
Southend-on-Sea
Redditch
Worcester
Hereford
Royal Leamington Spa
Northampton
Bedford
Milton Keynes
Luton
Stevenage
Hemel Hempstead
Harlow
Basildon
Cheltenham
Gloucester
Cotswold Hills
Oxford
High Wycombe
Watford
Slough
LONDON
Thames
Chatham
Maidstone
Canterbury
Margate
Dover
Reading
Newbury
Swindon
Bath
Bristol
Weston-super-Mare
Taunton
Exmoor
Barnstaple
Bude
618
Dartmoor
Newquay
Truro
St. Austell
Penzance
Land's End
Isles of Scilly
Falmouth
Plymouth
Torbay
Exmouth
Exeter
Yeovil
Weymouth
Poole
Bournemouth
Newport
Isle of Wight
Southampton
Winchester
Salisbury
Fareham
Havant
Portsmouth
Worthing
Brighton
Crawley
Guildford
Basingstoke
Reigate
Ashford
Folkestone
Hastings
Eastbourne

E n g l i s h   C h a n n e l

Str. of Dover
Boulogne-sur-Mer
Le Touquet-Paris-Plage
33

St. George's Channel
Fishguard
Haverfordwest
Milford Haven
Pembroke

NETHERLANDS
The Hague
Texel
Den Helder
Alkmaar
Haarlem
Hoek van Holland
ROTTERDAM
Dordrecht
Vlissingen
36
16
Zeebrugge
Oostende
Brugge
Antwerp
Gent
Mechelen
BELGIUM
BRUSSELS
Dunkerque
Calais
St.-Omer
Lille
Tournai
Tourcoing
Roubaix
Villeneuve d'Ascq
Béthune
Bruay-en-Artois
Lens
Valenciennes
Cambrai
St.-Quentin
Gris-Nez
C.

FRANCE
Alderney
C. de la Hague
Pte. de Barfleur
Cherbourg
Valognes
St. Peter Port
Guernsey
Sark
St. Helier
Jersey
Channel Is. (U.K.)
Bayeux
Caen
Lisieux
Elbeuf
Seine
Trouville-sur-Mer
Le Havre
Bolbec
Rouen
Fécamp
Abbeville
Le Tréport
Dieppe
Amiens
Pays de Caux
Picardie

West from Greenwich
East from Greenwich

Projection: Conical with two standard parallels

CARTOGRAPHY BY PHILIP'S.
COPYRIGHT REED INTERNATIONAL BOOKS LTD

1 : 5 000 000

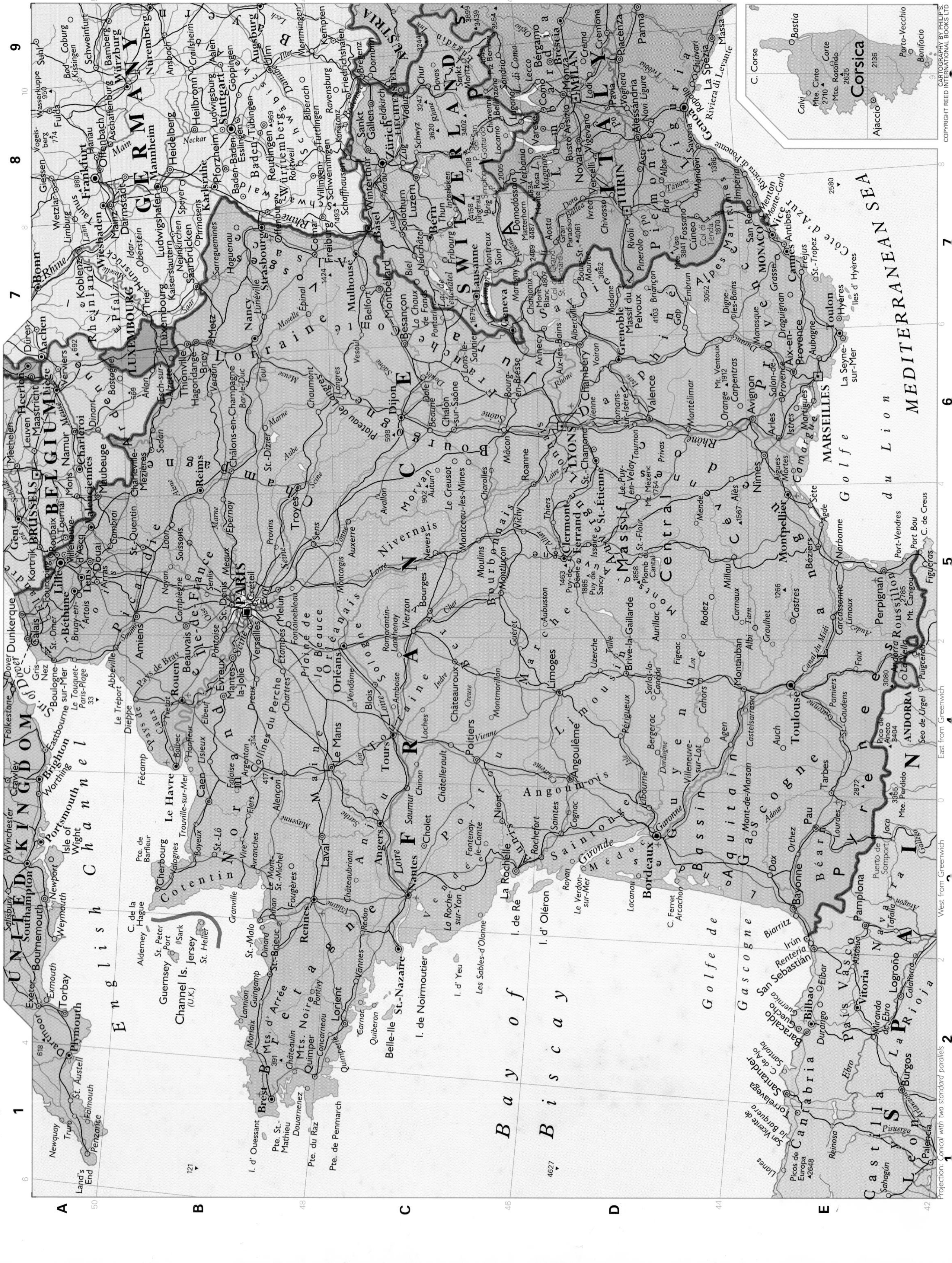

50   50   100 miles
50   50   100 150 km

CARTOGRAPHY BY PHILIP'S
COPYRIGHT REED INTERNATIONAL BOOKS LTD

Corsica
C. Corse
Calvi   Bastia
Mte. Cinto   Corte
2710   Rotondo
2625
Ajaccio   Porto-Vecchio
2136   Bonifacio

GERMANY
SWITZERLAND
AUSTRIA
ITALY
BELGIUM
LUXEMBOURG
UNITED KINGDOM
FRANCE
ANDORRA
MONACO

English Channel
Bay of Biscay
Golfe de Gascogne
MEDITERRANEAN SEA
Golfe du Lion

PARIS
MARSEILLES
LYONS
TURIN
MILAN
BRUSSELS

West from Greenwich   East from Greenwich

Projection: Conical with two standard parallels

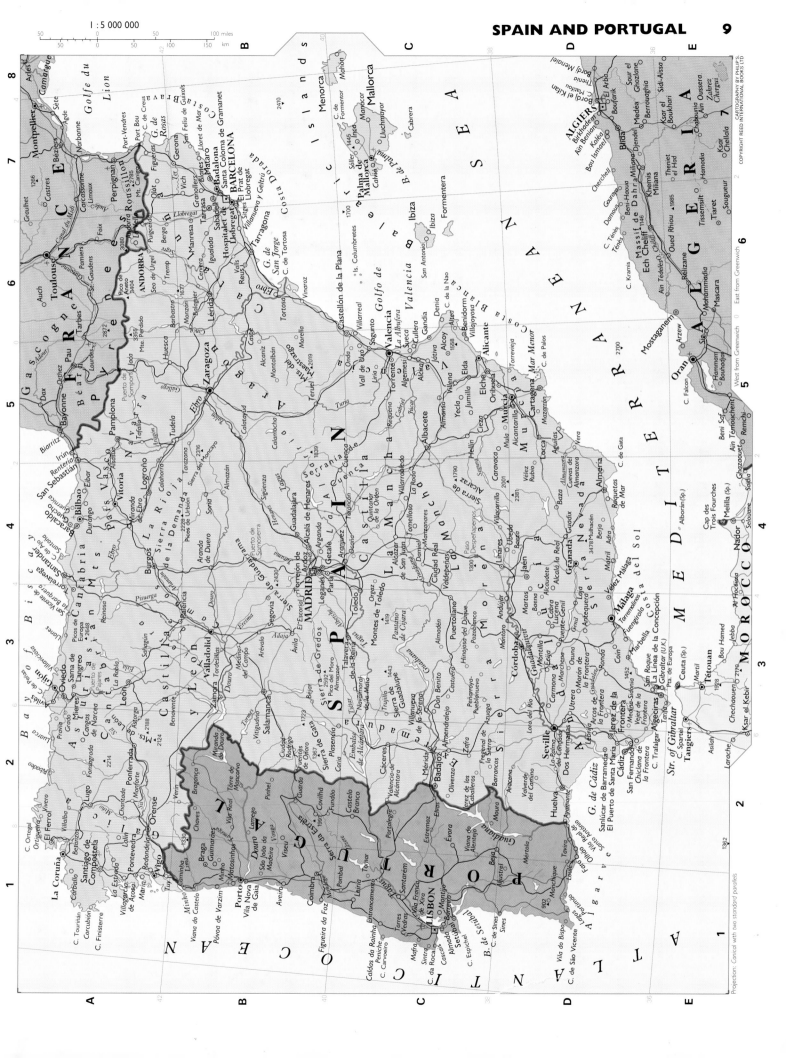

1 : 5 000 000

NORTH SEA

BALTIC SEA

DENMARK

UNITED KINGDOM

NETHERLANDS

GERMANY

BELGIUM

LUXEMBOURG

FRANCE

CZECH

SWITZERLAND

AUSTRIA

ITALY

SLOVENIA

ADRIATIC SEA

Vorkuta · Khalmer Yu · 1363 · Labytnangi · Salekhord · Berezovo · Ivdel · Sosva · Krasnoturinsk · Serov · Nizhniy Tagil · Sverdlovsk · YEKATERINBURG · Pervouralsk · Ufa · Miass · Zlatoust · Yaman Tau 1640 · Beloretsk · Novotroitsk · Orsk

Kholmer Yu · Usa · Inta · Narodnaya 1894 · Telpos Iz 1617 · Troitsko-Pechorsk · Kizel · Solikamsk 1869 · Berezniki · U R A L · Kungur · Nyazepetrovsk · BASHKORTOSTAN · Sterlitamak · Solovat · Kumertau · Orenburg

BOLSHEZEMELSK · Usa · Ust Usa · Arctic Circle · Pechora · Zheleznodorozhny · Ukhta · Cherdyn · Kama · Chusovoy · Lysva · PERM · Votkinsk · Birsk · Chernikovsk · UFA · Belaya · Sorochinsk

Naryan-Mar · G. of Pechora · Tundra · Ust Tsilma · Sosnogorsk · 463 · Mikun · Vychegda · Glazov · 337 · UDMURTIA · Izhevsk · Sarapul · Naberezhnyye Chelny · Kamb · Bugulma · Samara Reservoir · Buzuluk

Malozemelsk Tundra · Mezen · Karpogory · Pinega · Velikiy Ustyug · Syktyvkar · Koslan · Pinyug · Kotlas · Nolinsk · Kirov · V. Vyatka · Slobodskoy · MARI EL · Yoshkar Ola · CHUVASHIA · KAZAN · TATARSTAN · Kuybyshev · Dimitrovgrad · Togliatti · SAMARA · Novokuybyshevsk · Syzran · Volsk · Balakovo

Kolguyev · Chesha B. · Kanin Nos · Kanin Pen. · Mezen · Sharya · Sharya · Sharya · Kotelnich · Murashi · Neya · Vetluga · Volga · Alatyr · Simbirsk · Kuznetsk 351 ·

C. Kanin Nos · Onega · Onega · Drina Bay · Drina See. · Vels · Totma · Sukhona · Kostroma · Gorki Reservoir · Dzerzhinsk · Arzamas · MORDVINIA · Saransk · Morshansk · Penza · Serdobsk

White Sea · Severodvinsk · Arkhangelsk · Plesetsk · Nyandoma · Konosha · Kharovsk · Vologda · Gorki · Nizhniy Novgorod · Vladimir · Orekhovo-Zuyevo · Murom · Ryazan · Michurinsk · Lipetsk · Tambov

Kola Pen. · Dvina B. · G. of Onega · Vytegra · Belove L. · Cherepovets · Rybinsk Reservoir · Rybinsk · Yaroslavl · Rostov · Kimry · Sergiyev Posad · Kolomna · Podolsk · Novomoskovsk · Yelets

Murmansk · Monchegorsk · 1191 · L. Imandra · Kandalaksha G. · Kem · Belomorsk · L. Vyg · Povenets · Kondopoga L. · L. Onega · Podporozhye · Belozersk · Vyshniy Volochek · Tver · MOSCOW · Serpukhov · Tula · 293 · Kaluga · Bryansk · Orel

Rybachi Pen. · Kola B. · Pechenga · Alakurtti · Kandalaksha · Pya L. · Kuito Ls. · 417 L. Seg · Medvezhyegorsk · Petrozavodsk · Olonets · Syas · Lodeinoye Pole · Novaya Ladoga · Borovichi · 343 · Vyazma · Smolensk · Roslavl

L. Inari · L. Top L. · Kemi · KARELIA · Sortavala · L. Ladoga · Priozersk · Neva · ST. PETERSBURG · Leningrad · Novgorod · Staraya Russa · Velikiye Luki · Valdai Hills · Volga · Rzhev · Vitebsk · Mogilev · Smolensk

Kemijärvi · Kemi · Yensijoki · Savonlinna · Vyborg · Kotka · L. Saimaa · Volkhov · L. Ilmen · Pskov · Velikaya · Orsha · Dnieper · 346 · MINSK · Bobruysk · Gomel · Chernikov

Kebnekaise 2117 · Kiruna · Gällivare · Kemi · Oulu · FINLAND · Lahti · Tampere · Helsinki · G. of Finland · Tallinn · ESTONIA · L. Chudskoye · Tartu · Luga · Pskov · LATVIA · Riga · Borisov · BELARUS · Baranovichi · Pripet Marshes · Pinsk · Pripet

Narvik · Torne L. · Gällivare · Kalix · Luleå · Vaasa · Pori · Turku · Aland Is. (Ahvenanmaa) · Hiiumaa · Saaremaa · G. of Riga · Pärnu · Jelgava · Daugava · Daugavpils · 346 · LITHUANIA · Siauliai · Vilnius · Grodno · Bialystok · Brest · Bug · WARSAW · POLAND

NORWAY · SWEDEN · Bodø · Mo · 1915 · Umeå · Ume · Angerman · Sundsvall · Soderhamn · Stockholm · Gulf of Bothnia · Ventspils · Liepaja · Klaipeda · Sovetsk · KALININGRAD · Kaunas · Neman · (RUSSIA) · Lomza · Lublin

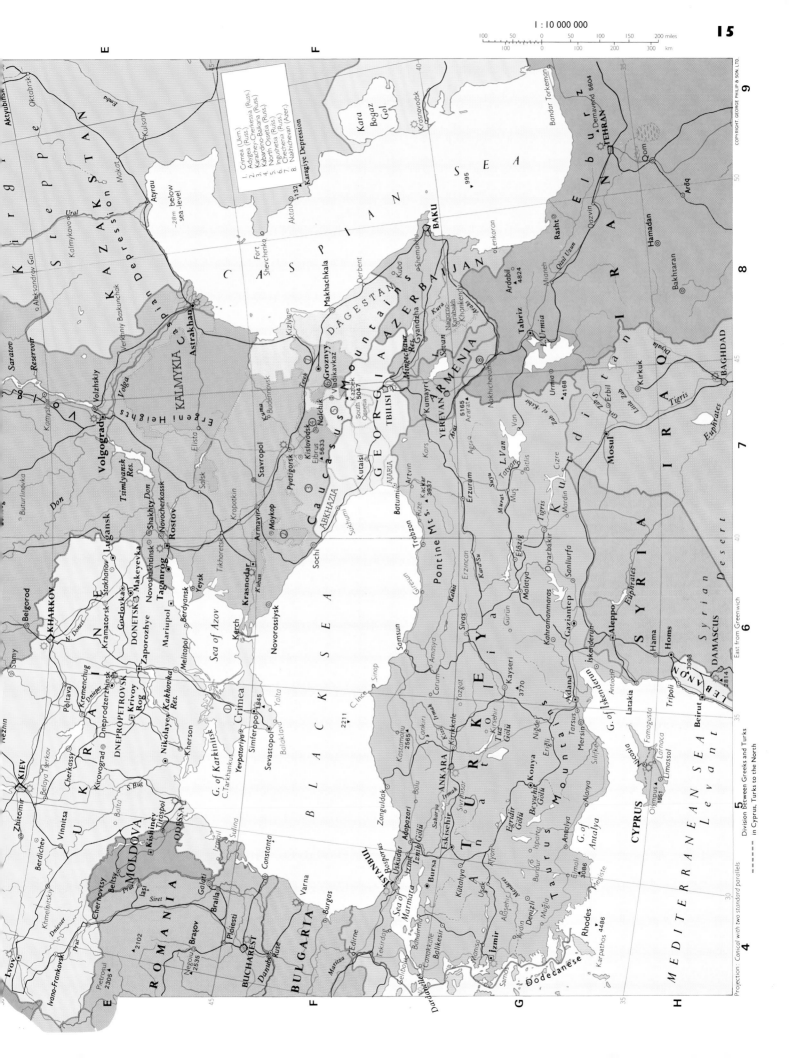

1 : 50 000 000

250   0   250   500   750   1000 miles
250   0   500   1000   1500 km

CARTOGRAPHY BY PHILIPS.COPYRIGHT REED INTERNATIONAL BOOKS LTD.

PACIFIC OCEAN

ARCTIC OCEAN

ATLANTIC OCEAN

INDIAN OCEAN

South China Sea

Arabian Sea

Bay of Bengal

Caspian Sea

Black Sea

Mediterranean Sea

Red Sea

The Gulf

Europe

Africa

Siberia

West Siberian Plain

Central Siberian Plateau

Plateau of Tibet

Himalaya

Kunlun Shan

Tian Shan

Hindu Kush

Plateau of Iran

Arabia

Mesopotamia

Middle East

Scandinavia

North European Plain

Ural Mts.

Steppe

Libyan Desert

Projection: Bonne 30

ft   m
4000
3000
2000
1000
500
200
0

ft   12000   9000   6000   3000   1500   600   0   200 600   1600 3000   6600 12000   4000 6000   12000 18000   24 000
m   600   3000   6000   18 000   m

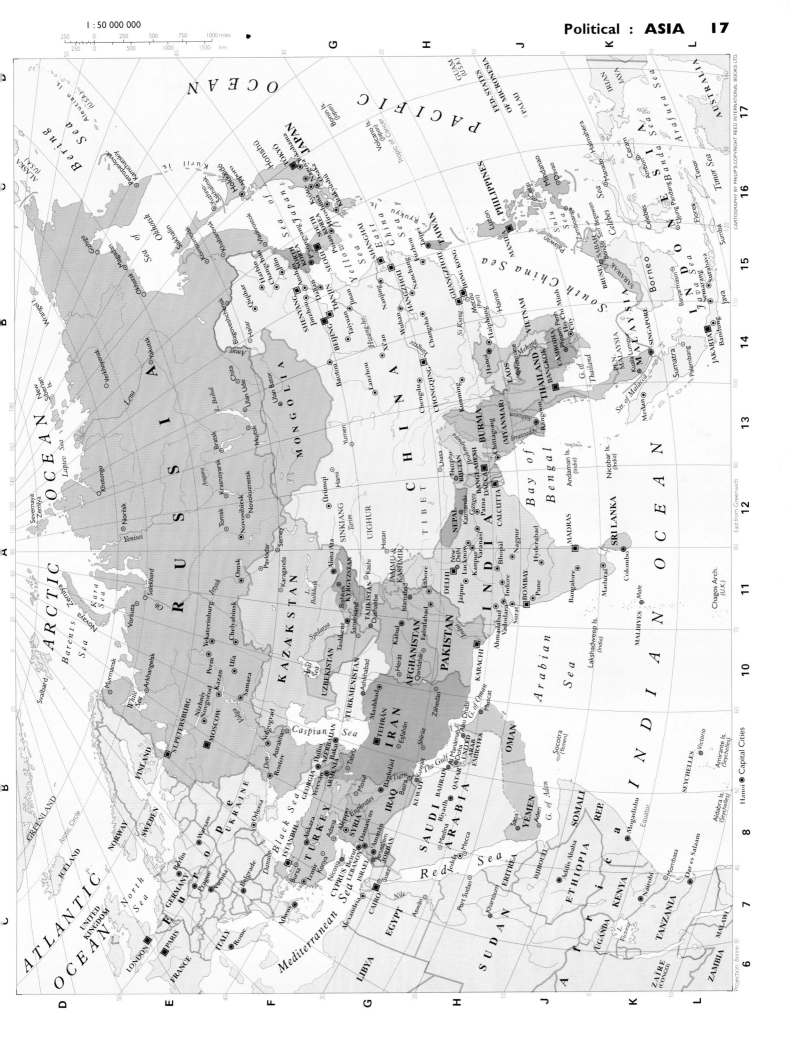

1 : 50 000 000

250   0   250   500   750   1000 miles
50   0   500   1000   1500   km

CARTOGRAPHY BY PHILIP'S COPYRIGHT REED INTERNATIONAL BOOKS LTD.

PACIFIC OCEAN

ATLANTIC OCEAN

ARCTIC OCEAN

INDIAN OCEAN

Bering Sea

Sea of Okhotsk

Sea of Japan

Yellow Sea

East China Sea

South China Sea

Philippine Sea

Celebes Sea

Sulu Sea

Java Sea

Banda Sea

Arafura Sea

Timor Sea

Flores Sea

Bay of Bengal

Arabian Sea

Red Sea

Mediterranean Sea

Black Sea

Caspian Sea

Aral Sea

Barents Sea

Kara Sea

Laptev Sea

White Sea

North Sea

The Gulf

G. of Oman

G. of Aden

G. of Thailand

Str. of Malacca

RUSSIA

CHINA

MONGOLIA

KAZAKSTAN

INDIA

IRAN

SAUDI ARABIA

PAKISTAN

AFGHANISTAN

TURKMENISTAN

UZBEKISTAN

KYRGYZSTAN

TAJIKISTAN

JAPAN

NORTH KOREA

SOUTH KOREA

TAIWAN

PHILIPPINES

INDONESIA

MALAYSIA

THAILAND

VIETNAM

LAOS

CAMBODIA

BURMA (MYANMAR)

BANGLADESH

NEPAL

BHUTAN

SRI LANKA

IRAQ

SYRIA

TURKEY

JORDAN

ISRAEL

LEBANON

CYPRUS

OMAN

YEMEN

UNITED ARAB EMIRATES

QATAR

BAHRAIN

KUWAIT

GEORGIA

ARMENIA

AZERBAIJAN

EGYPT

SUDAN

LIBYA

ETHIOPIA

ERITREA

DJIBOUTI

SOMALI REP.

KENYA

TANZANIA

UGANDA

ZAIRE (CONGO)

ZAMBIA

MALAWI

FINLAND

SWEDEN

NORWAY

UNITED KINGDOM

FRANCE

GERMANY

ITALY

ICELAND

GREENLAND

UKRAINE

POLAND

Europe

Africa

AUSTRALIA

ALASKA (U.S.A.)

SINKIANG UIGHUR

TIBET

JAMMU & KASHMIR

MALDIVES

SEYCHELLES

Chagos Arch. (U.K.)

Lakshadweep Is. (India)

Andaman Is. (India)

Nicobar Is. (India)

Aldabra Is. (Seychelles)

Amirante Is. (Seychelles)

Borneo

Sumatra

Java

Luzon

Mindanao

Hainan

Taiwan

Hokkaido

Honshu

Shikoku

Kyushu

Sakhalin

Kuril Is.

Sri Lanka

Svalbard

Novaya Zemlya

Severnaya Zemlya

New Siberian Is.

Wrangel I.

Socotra (Yemen)

Aleutian Is. (USA)

Volcano Is. (Japan)

Ryukyu Is.

Palawan

Ceram

Ambon

Halmahera

Celebes

Sumba

Timor

Ljung Pandang

GUAM (USA)

FEDERATED STATES OF MICRONESIA

PALAU

IRIAN

Tropic of Cancer

Arctic Circle

Equator

East from Greenwich

Projection: Bonne 30

● TOKYO
● BEIJING
● SEOUL
● PYONGYANG
● MOSCOW
● ST. PETERSBURG
● NEW DELHI
● TEHRAN
● BAGHDAD
● RIYADH
● ISTANBUL
● ANKARA
● CAIRO
● LONDON
● PARIS
● BERLIN
● PRAGUE
● ROME
● WARSAW
● BUDAPEST
● VIENNA
● BELGRADE
● MANILA
● HANOI
● BANGKOK
● RANGOON
● DACCA
● CALCUTTA
● BOMBAY
● MADRAS
● KARACHI
● SHANGHAI
● GUANGZHOU
● HONG KONG
● WUHAN
● CHONGQING
● JAKARTA
● SINGAPORE
● KUALA LUMPUR
● PHNOM PENH
● HO CHI MINH CITY
● VIENTIANE
● BANDAR SERI BEGAWAN
● KABUL
● ISLAMABAD
● ASHKHABAD
● TASHKENT
● BISHKEK
● DUSHANBE
● ALMA-ATA
● BAKU
● TBILISI
● YEREVAN
● KATHMANDU
● THIMPHU
● COLOMBO
● MALE
● VICTORIA

Cities (selected): Yakutsk, Verkhoyansk, Magadan, Petropavlovsk, Kamchatsky, Khabarovsk, Vladivostok, Komsomolsk, Nikolayevsk, Irkutsk, Ulan Ude, Chita, Bratsk, L. Baykal, Krasnoyarsk, Novosibirsk, Novokuznetsk, Tomsk, Omsk, Pavlodar, Semey, Karaganda, Norilsk, Khatanga, Igarka, Salekhard, Vorkuta, Yekaterinburg, Perm, Ufa, Chelyabinsk, Kazan, Samara, Volgograd, Saratov, Astrakhan, Rostov, Murmansk, Arkhangelsk, Nizhniy Novgorod, Yenisei, Ob, Irtysh, Lena, Amur, Angara, Volga, Don, Syrdarya, Ural

China cities: Harbin, Qiqihar, Changchun, Jilin, Shenyang, Dalian, Jinzhou, Tianjin, Taiyuan, Baotou, Lanzhou, Xi'an, Chengdu, Kunming, Nanjing, Hangzhou, Hefei, Nanchang, Fuzhou, Xiamen, Changsha, Guiyang, Nanning, Haikou, Macau, Hohhot, Yumen, Hami, Ürümqi, Kashi, Hotan, Lhasa, Qingdao

India cities: Jaipur, Lucknow, Kanpur, Varanasi, Patna, Ahmadabad, Vadodara, Surat, Indore, Bhopal, Nagpur, Hyderabad, Pune, Bangalore, Madurai

Middle East cities: Mashhad, Esfahan, Shiraz, Zahedan, Qandahar, Herat, Tabriz, Mosul, Basra, Kuwait, Al Manamah, Doha, Abu Dhabi, Muscat, Sana, Aden, Medina, Mecca, Jedda, Aswan, Alexandria, Port Said, Suez, Nile, Tigris, Euphrates, Aleppo, Adana, Konya, Bursa, Nicosia, Beirut, Damascus, Amman, Jerusalem, Athens, Sofia, Odessa, Kiev, Danube

Africa cities: Khartoum, Port Sudan, Addis Ababa, Mogadishu, Nairobi, L. Victoria, Mombasa, Dar es Salaam

SE Asia: Medan, Palembang, Bandung, Surabaya, Banjarmasin, Semarang, Manado, Davao, Cebu, Zamboanga, Kuching, Kota Kinabalu, Chittagong, Mandalay, Irrawaddy, Salween, Mekong, Si Kiang, Brahmaputra, Ganges, Haiphong, Haikou

Hanoi ● Capital Cities

1 : 35 000 000

200   0   200   400   600   800 miles

400   0   400   800   1200 km

ARCTIC OCEAN

Bering Sea

Gulf of Anadyr

Lawrence I. (U.S.)

Near Is. (U.S.)

Komandorskiye

Kamchatka

Chukot Ra.

Sredinny Ra.

Gulf of Shelikhov

Sea of Okhotsk

Kolyma Ra.

Cherski Ra.

Verkhoyansk Ra.

Central Siberian Plateau

Taimyr Peninsula

Severnaya Zemlya

New Siberian Is.

East Siberian Sea

Wrangel I.

Laptev Sea

Kara Sea

Novaya Zemlya

Barents Sea

Svalbard (Spitsbergen)

Franz Josef Land

Kolguyev I.

White Sea

Kola Pen.

Arctic Circle

Norwegian Sea

North Sea

NORWAY   SWEDEN   FINLAND

Trondheim   Bergen   Oslo   Stockholm   Helsinki   Tampere

DENMARK   Copenhagen   Edinburgh   UNITED KINGDOM

Hamburg   GERMANY   Berlin   POLAND   Warsaw

ESTONIA   LATVIA   LITHUANIA   Riga   Tallinn   Vilnius

Kaliningrad (Russia)   BELARUS   Minsk

Murmansk   Arkhangelsk

St. Petersburg   MOSCOW   Yaroslavl   Rybinsk   Tver

Smolensk   Orel   Tula   Ryazan

Nizhniy Novgorod   Kirov   Izhevsk   Perm   Ufa   Kazan

Nizhny Tagil   Yekaterinburg   Chelyabinsk   Kurgan

Serov   Tyumen   Omsk

Samara   Orenburg   Magnitogorsk

Saratov   Penza   Tambov   Voronezh   Kursk

Volgograd   Astrakhan

UKRAINE   Kiev   Kharkov   Dnepropetrovsk   Krivoy Rog   Nikolayev

Odessa   MOLDOVA   ROMANIA

Black Sea   Sevastopol   Rostov   Krasnodar

Caspian Sea   Baku   AZERBAIJAN   ARMENIA   GEORGIA   Tbilisi   Yerevan

TURKEY   Baghdad   Mosul   Tigris   Euphrates

IRAN   Tehran   Mashhad   Tabriz   Esfahan   Yazd   Shiraz   Ahvaz   Abadan

Elburz Mts.   Zagros Mts.

The Gulf   BAHRAIN   QATAR   UNITED ARAB EMIRATES   OMAN   KUWAIT   Basra

Gulf of Oman

KAZAKHSTAN   Karaganda   Alma Ata   Aqmola   Semey   Pavlodar

Aral Sea   L. Balkhash   Kzyl Orda

UZBEKISTAN   Tashkent   Samarkand   TURKMENISTAN   Ashkhabad

Kyzyl Kum   Kara Kum   Ust Urt Plateau   Amudarya   Syrdarya

KYRGYZSTAN   Bishkek   TAJIKISTAN   Dushanbe

AFGHANISTAN   Kabul   Herat   Qondahar   Mashhad

Hindu Kush   PAKISTAN   Peshawar   Islamabad   Rawalpindi   Lahore   Quetta

INDIA   Delhi   Meerut   Amritsar   Ludhiana   Srinagar

Himalaya   Karakoram   K2   Kunlun Shan   TIBET

Takla Makan   Tarim   SINKIANG-UIGHUR

Tien Shan   Ala Shan   Nan Shan

Urumqi   Turpan   Dzungaria

MONGOLIA   Ulan Bator   Great Khingan Mts.

Novosibirsk   Omsk   Tomsk   Kemerovo   Novokuznetsk   Barnaul   Biysk

Krasnoyarsk   Kansk   Irkutsk   Ulan Udey   Chita

West Siberian Plain

Ural Mountains

Yenisey   Lena   Ob   Angara

Yablonovyy Ra.   Stanovoy Ra.   Dzhugdzhur Ra.

Amur   Komsomolsk   Blagoveshchensk   Khabarovsk   Vladivostok

Sikhote Alin Ra.   Sakhalin

KOREA   Seoul   Pyongyang   Dalian

Yellow Sea   East China Sea   Sea of Japan

JAPAN   Hokkaido   Honshu   Shikoku   Kyushu   TOKYO   Yokohama   Kobe   Kyoto   Osaka   Nagoya   Sapporo

Kuril Is.

CHINA   BEIJING   Tianjin   Taiyuan   Xi'an   Lanzhou   Chengdu   Chongqing   Wuhan   SHANGHAI   Nanjing   Hangzhou   Nanchang   Changsha   Guangzhou   Fuzhou   Xiamen

Hwang-ho   Yangtze Kiang   Mekong   Salween

TAIWAN   Taipei

Tropic of Cancer

East from Greenwich

Projection: Lambert's Conical Orthomorphic

COPYRIGHT GEORGE PHILIP & SON LTD.

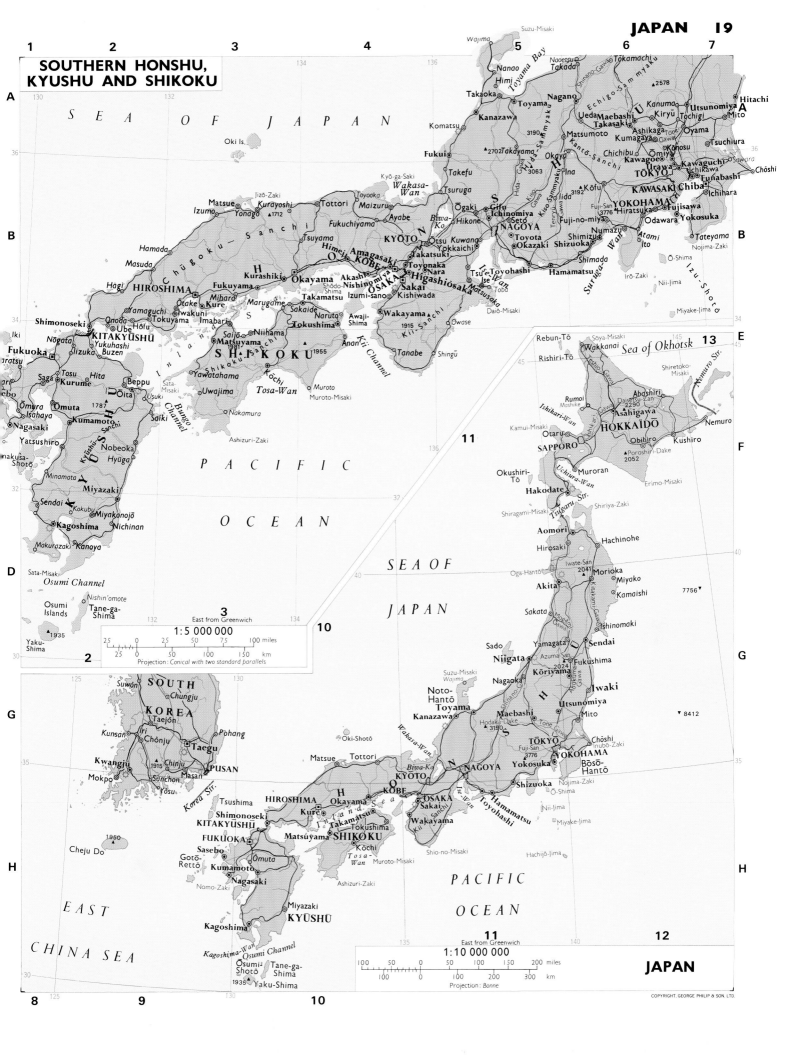

1   2   3   4   5

50

K A Z A K S T A N

Karsakpay
Karaganda
Karkaralinsk
1565
Rubtsovsk
Semey
Öskeman
70   80
Irtysh
Western Sayan
RUSSIA
Cheremkhovo
Angarsk
Irkutsk
455
Belukha 4506
Zyryanovsk
Khuken
Munku Sardyk 3491
Tannu Ola
Hövsgöl Nuur
Hatgal

B
342
Lake Balkhash
Taldy-Kurgan
Ayaguz
Lake Zaisan
Tarbagatai Ra.
Fuhai
Altay
Uvs Nuur
Har Us Nuur
Hovd
4362
Ulaangom
Hyargas Nuur
DörÖÖ Nuur Ulyosutay
Khangai
Tsetserleg
Ulan Bator
Dzuunmod

Chu
Ala Tau
Ala Kul
Tacheng
Fuyun
A l t a i
Buyanhongor
Dalandzadgad

Bishkek
Dzhambul
Issyk-Kul
1609
KYRGYZSTAN
Namangan
Andizhan
Yining
Ili
Bole
Dzungarian Gates
Usu
Karamay
Ulungur
Qitai
D z u n g a r i a
T i a n   S h a n
Ürümqi 5445
4925
Hami
Gaxun Nur
Gobi

40
Pik Pobedy 7439
Naryn
Kashi
Aksu
Kuqa
Korla
Bosten (Bagrax) Hu
Kuruktag
SINKIANG UIGHUR
Shache
1635
Yecheng
Hotan
Yutian
Qiemo
Ruoqiang
Tarim He
Tarim Basin
Lop Nor
Dunhuang
Anxi
Yumen
Jiayuguan
Ala Shan
Alxa Zuoqi
Wuhai
1251
Zhangye
NINGXIA HUIZU
Yincluan
Wuzhong

Takla Makan
Altun Shan
Da Qaidam
6346
Nan Shan
Tianjun
Wuwei
ZIZHIQU

C
8126
Karakoram
K2 8611
Karakoram Pass
5575
JAMMU & KASHMIR
Srinagar
Leh
Rutog
7723
K u n l u n   S h a n
Qaidam Pendi
Golmud
Da Qaidam
Dulan
Qinghai Hu 3205
Gonghe
Xining
Linxia
LANZHOU
Pingliang

Gar
Nanda Devi 7817
Burang
Dehra Dun
Mapam Yumco
Zhongba
Xainza
T I B E T
Siling Co 4495
Tanglha Range
Amdo
Nagqu
Nam Co 4627
Nyenchen Tanglha Range
Lhasa
Namcha Barwa 7756
Bomi
Yarlung Zangbo
Lhaze
Xigaze
Yamzho Yumco
Ngoring Hu 4237
Gyaring Hu
Maqen
6094
Yushu
Amdo
Hoang-ho
Mekong
Yangtze
Qamdo
Garze
Zayü
Shaluli Shan
Ninging Shan
(Lancang Jiang)
Bayan Har Shan
QINGHAI
Min Xian
Tianshui
Baoji
Wudu
4113
Hanzhong

C
30
Meerut
DELHI
Moradabad
Bareilly
Aligarh
Agra
KANPUR
Gwalior
LUCKNOW
Gorakhpur
Dhaulagiri 8221
NEPAL
Katmandu
Everest 8848
H i m a l a y a
Koch Bihar
Thimphu
BHUTAN
Dibrugarh
Gauhati
Tezpur
Patkar Hills 3411
5881
Zhongdian
Lijiang
Xiaguan
Daxue Shan
Gongga Shan 7600
SICHUAN
Mianyang
Daxian
CHENGDU
Neijiang
Zigong
Yibin
Luzhou
Wutongqiao
Nanchong
Hechuan
CHONGQ
(Chungk)
Yangtze

D
Jhansi
Allahabad
Varanasi
Patna
Ganges
I N D I A
Gorakhpur
Rajshahi
BANGLADESH
Khasi Hills
Khulna
Imphal 3824
Silchar
Myitkyina
Bhamo
Baoshan
Luxi
Xichang
Dongchuan
Zhaotong
Zunyi
Wu
GUIZH
Guiyan
Duy

Tropic of Cancer
Jabalpur
Ranchi
Jamshedpur
Asansol
Haora
CALCUTTA
DACCA (Dhaka)
Narayanganj
CHITTAGONG
Bangladesh
Monywa
Victoria 3053
Mandalay
2650
3143
VIETNAM
HANOI
HAIPHONG
Gulf of
Tonkin
KUNMING
Xingyi
Shiping
Gejiu
Wenshan
Hongshui
Hechi
Nanning
Pingxiang
Qinzhe
ZHU
YUNNAN
Jiangcheng
Song Da (Black)
Hong Ha
Red

E
Warangal
Vishakhapatnam
Raipur
Nagpur
Mahanadi
Cuttack
Indravati
BAY OF BENGAL
Akyab
Arakan Yoma
Pegu Yoma
Irrawaddy
Yamethin
Toungoo
2163
THAILAND
Salween
Mekong
LAOS
Hoa-binh
Luang Prabang
BURMA (MYANMAR)

20

Projection: Bonne   East from Greenwich

80   3   90   4   100   5

1 : 20 000 000

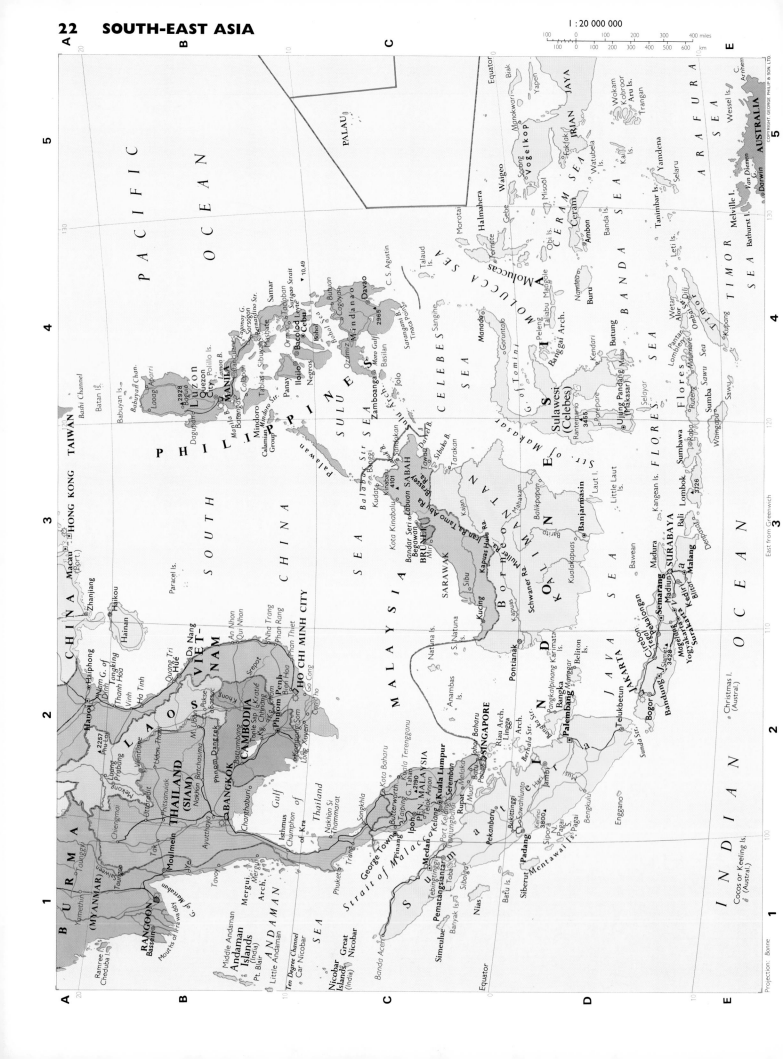

COPYRIGHT GEORGE PHILIP & SON, LTD.

Projection: Bonne

East from Greenwich

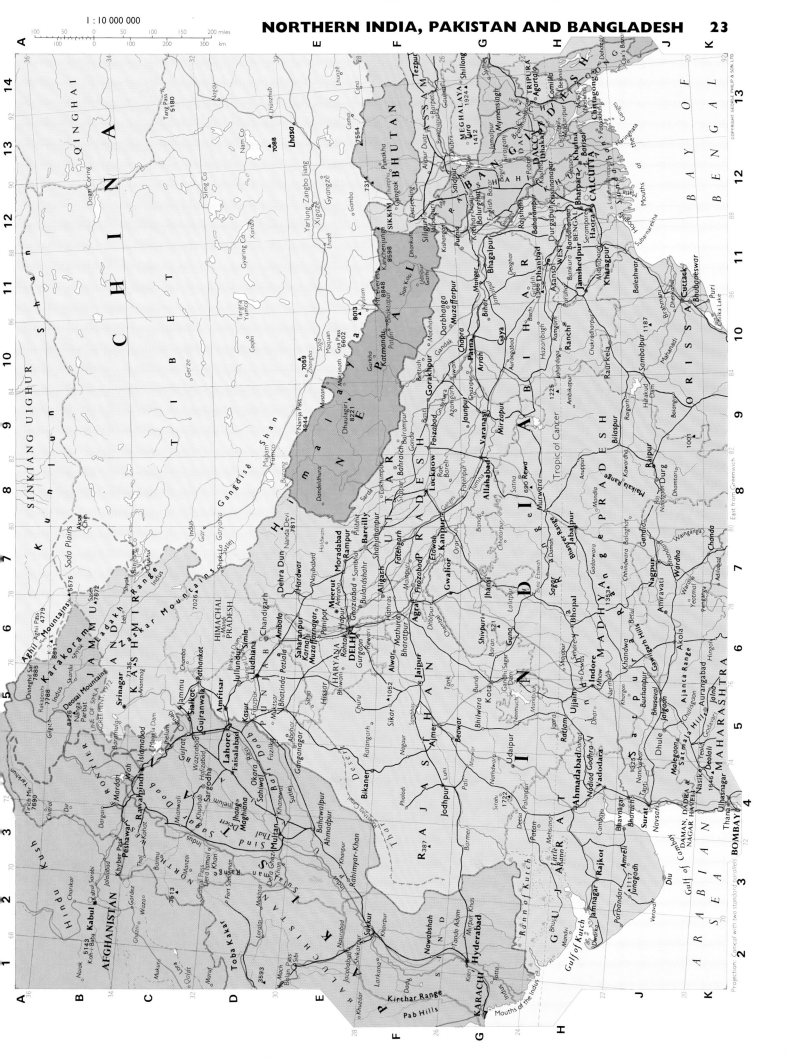

1   2   3   4   5

B

C

D

E

TURKEY
Konya
Kayseri
Malatya
Erzurum
Adana
Mersin
Gaziantep
Diyarbakir
Elâziğ
Kumayri Gyandzha
Yerevan ARMENIA
AZERBAIJAN
Baku
KAZAKHSTAN

Taurus
Bitlis
L. Van
Mus

Kara Bogaz Gol
Caspian Sea
Krasnovodsk

UZBEKISTAN
Urgench
Amudarya
Bukhara
Sa

CYPRUS
Nicosia
Tripoli
Latakia
Aleppo (Halab)
Hama
SYRIA
Homs

Mosul
Kurdistan
Tabriz
Urmia
Ardabil
Lenkoran
Anzali
Rasht
Babol
Elburz Mountains
Ashkhabad

TURKMENISTAN
Kara Kum
Chardzhou
Mary
Bairam-Ali Ke
Te

LEBANON
Beirut
Damascus

Euphrates
Mesopotamia
Erbil
Kirkuk
Zanjan
Qazvin
Hamadan
Qom
Tehran
Damavend 5604

Mashhad

Mazar-e Sharif
Maimana
Herat

ISRAEL
Haifa
Tel Aviv-Jaffa
Alexandria
Damanhur
Mansura
Dumyât
Tanta
Port Said
Ismailia
Cairo
El Faiyum
Suez

Amman
Jerusalem
JORDAN
Dead Sea
Ma'an

Syrian Desert
Ar Ramadi
Karbala
Baghdad
Hilla
Al Kut
An Najaf
An Nasiriyah

IRAQ

Bakhtaran
Araq
Kashan
Esfahan
4648
Yazd

IRAN
Dasht-e-Lut
Tabas
Gonabad
Birjand

AFGHANISTAN
Farah
Farah
Girishk
Qandahar

Sinai
2637

Arabian Desert
Red Sea

Qena
Luxor
Qûs
Bûr Safâga
Quseir

HEJAZ
Al'Ula
Hail

Nafud Desert
Turabah
Buraydah

Basra
Khorramshahr
Abadan
Bandar Khomeyni

KUWAIT
Kuwait

Ahvaz
Shiraz
Kazerun
Busher

Shatt al Arab

Kerman
Zahedan
Saidabad
4078

PAKI
Quetta
Nushki
Shikarp

Ras Banas
Yenbo
Medina
Rabigh

SAUDI ARABIA
Mubarraz
Riyadh
Al-Hufuf

Dammam
BAHRAIN
QATAR
Doha
Sharjah
Dubai
Abu Dhabi

Gulf
The Gulf of Oman
Bandar Abbas
Str. of Hormuz
Jask
As Sohar

Gwadar
Ormara
Pasni
Dashti
Central Makran Ra.
Bela
Nawab

Karachi
Indus Delt
Tropic of Cancer

Jedda
Mecca
Taif
2259

'Asir

UNITED ARAB EMIRATES
Layla
Sulaiyil
Abha

Rub' al Khali
(Empty Quarter)

Hajar
3048
Muscat
OMAN
Ras al Hadd

Port Sudan
Suakin
Haiya
Halaib

SUDAN

Mesewa
Dahlak Arch.
Asmera
ERITREA
Al Hudaydah
116
Ta'izz
Mussa
2063
Bab el Mandeb

Farasan Is.

Amran
Sana'
Marib
Shibam
Hadhramaut
YEMEN
Madinat al Shaab
Aden
Shuqra
Mukalla
Sayhut

Ras Fartak

G. of Masirah
Ras al Madraka
Kuria Muria Is.
Mirbat

ARABIAN

Dese

ETHIOPIA
Dire Dawa
Harer
Hargeisa
Gabredarre

DJIBOUTI
Djibouti
Gulf of Aden
Berbera
Erigavo
Ras Asir
(C. Guardafui)
Hordio

Socotra
(Yemen)

SEA

SOMALI REP.
Juba
Shibeli
Mogadishu
Obbia
Ilig
Bender Beila

I N D I A

East from Greenwich

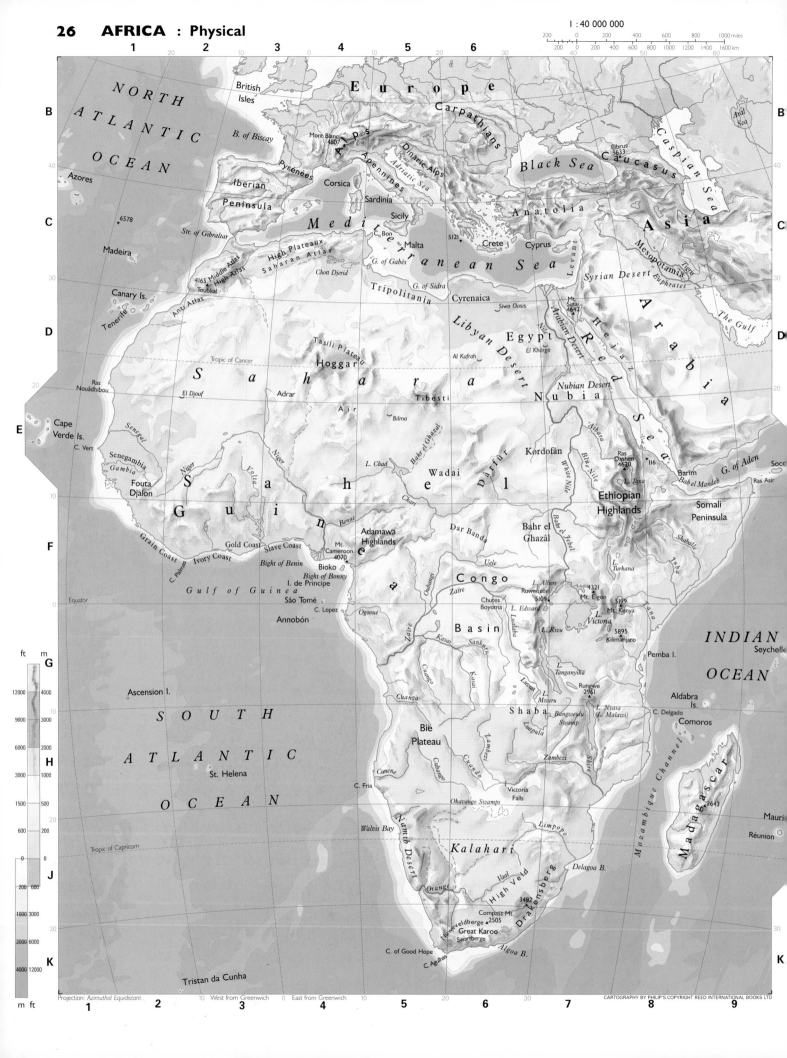

NORTH ATLANTIC

OCEAN

Madeira (Port.)
Funchal
Pto. Santo

6578

SPAIN
Cádiz · Málaga · Almería
Gibraltar (U.K.)
Str. of Gibraltar
Tangier · Ceuta (Sp.)
Tétouan · Al Hoceima
Larache · Melilla (Sp.)
Ksar el Kebir
Ouezzane
Kenitra · Fès · Taza
Salé · Oujda
Rabat · Meknès
Casablanca
El Jadida · Berrechid
Settat · Khouribga
Safi · Beni Mellal
MOROCCO
Essaouira · Marrakesh
Ar Rachidya
Dj. Toubkal ▲ 4165
C. Rhir
Agadir · Taroudannt · Ouarzazate
Anti Atlas
Ifni · Tiznit
Dra
Bou Izakarn
Tan-Tan
Tindouf

CANARY IS. (Sp.)
La Palma
Tenerife · Lanzarote
Gomera 3718 · Fuerteventura · Arrecife
Hierro · Sta. Cruz · Puerto del Rosario
Gran Canaria · Las Palmas
C. Juby · Tarfaya
El Aaiún
Semara
Bu Craa
C. Bojador
Dakhla
C. Barbas

WESTERN SAHARA
Féderik
Bir Mogrein
Aïn Ben Tili
Zouérate
Chegga

Mostaganem · Ech Cheliff · Algiers · Tizi-Ouzou · Bejaïa · Skikda · Annaba
Sidi-Bel-Abbès · Blida · Constantine · Guelma
Oran · Médéa · Sétif · Batna
Ghazaouet · Tlemcen · Saïda · Bou Saâda · Khenchela · Aïn Beïda
TUNISIA
Tiaret · Djelfa · Biskra · Tolga · Nefta
Mecheria · El Bayadh · Laghouat · Touggourt · El Oued · Gabès
Bouârfa · Figuig · Ghardaïa · Hassi er Rmel · El Oued
Beni Ounif · Ouargla · Hassi Messaoud
Béchar · Ghudamis
Abadla · Beni Abbès · Timimoun · Hassi Inifel · Ghdames
Igli · Ft. Mac-Mahon · Ft. Miribel
Kerzaz · Charouine · In Belbel · In Salah · Ohanet
Adrar · Miliana · Bordj Omar Driss
ALGERIA
Bj. Fly Ste. Marie · Aoulef el Arab · Illizi
Zaouïet Reggane · Bj.-Tarat
Arak · Sardalas
Ouallene · Ghat
Bj.-in-Eker · Idelès
Erg Chech · Tahat ▲ 2918 · Hoggar · Djanet

Terhazza · Tanezrouft · Tamanrasset
Taoudenni · Poste Maurice Cortier · Admer
MAURITANIA
Chår · Ouadâne
Atâr · Chinguetti
Ouleit · El Djouf
Akjoujt · Rachid · Tidjikja · Mabrouk · Aïr · Monts Tamgak
Nouakchott · Tichît · Araouane · Bou Djébéha · Iférouâne · 1900
Boutilimit · Akreijit · Kidal · I-n-Gall · Abalésa
Mederdra · Aleg · Togba · Tâmchekket · Bamba · Kerchoual · Agadez
Kiffa · Néma · Goundam · Diré · Gourma-Rharous
St. Louis · Ras Timiris · Moudjéria · Oualâta · Tombouctou · Gaô · Ménaka · NIGER
Tivaouane · Podor · Kaédi · Timbedgha · Kabara · Ansongo · Tahoua · Tanout
Rufisque · Dagana · M'bout · Nioro du Sahel · Niafouké · Hombori · Filingué · Tamaské · Boultoum
C. Vert · Thiès · Louga · Linguère · Sélibabi · Nara · Ménaka · Madaoua · Zinder · Kellé
Dakar · Kaolack · Matam · Dahra · Yélimané · MALI · Douentza · Famalé · Birni Nkonni · Maradi · Nguru
SENEGAL · Kaffrine · Diel · Mourdiah · Sokolo · Mopti · Djibo · Téra · Tillabéri · Kamaguérin · Goursél
Banjul · Tambacounda · Bakel · Didiéni · Sagala · Bandiagara · BURKINA · Dori · Niamey · Sokoto · Tessaoua
GAMBIA · Georgetown · Kayes · Ké-Macina · Ségou · Djenné · FASO · Ouahigouya · Dosso · Argungu · Gusau · Kano
Ziguinchor · Kolda · Satadougou · Kita · Koulikoro · Sarro · Toma · Yako · N'Gourma · Birni Kebbi · Hadejia
Bissau · Bafatá · Dinguiraye · Bamako · Douna · Koutiala · Ouagadougou · Fada · Jega · Zaria
GUINEA-BISSAU · Gaoual · Siguiri · Bougouni · Sikasso · Bobo-Dioulasso · Koudougou · Tenkodogo · Kandi · NIGERIA
Bâlama · Fouta Djalon · Tougué · Bananba · Léo · Tumu · Magoro · Bembéré · Kaduna
GUINEA · Dabola · Kankan · Banfora · Diébougou · Gaoua · Mango · Parakou · Minna · Jos
Conakry · Forécariah · Kabala · Bissidougou · Faranah · Odienné · Boundiali · Tawra · Natitingou · Nikki · Kabba · Shendam
SIERRA LEONE · 1948 · Guéckédou · Macenta · Touba · Séguéla · Bouaké · BENIN · Tamale · Shaki · Ilorin · Lafia
Freetown · Makeni · Magburaka · Man · Danané · IVORY COAST · Katiola · Bondoukou · GHANA · Salaga · TOGO · Ogbomosho · Oyo · Makurdi
Waterloo · Moyamba · Bo · Kenema · Gagnoa · Daloa · Lake Volta · Ibadan · Iwo · Oshogbo · Enugu
Sherbro · Bonthe · Tapeta · COAST · Bocanda · Yamoussoukro · Kumasi · Cotonou · Abeokuta · Ondo · Benin City · Onitsha
LIBERIA · Toulepleu · Dimbokro · Obuasi · Kpalimé · Porto-Novo · Lagos · Sapele · CAMEROON
Monrovia · Marshall · Tiassalé · Prestea · Tema · Accra · Lomé · Bight of Benin · Mt. Cameroon 4070 ▲ · Douala
Buchanan · River Cess · Grabo · Sekondi-Takoradi · Cape Coast · Port Harcourt · Aba · Calabar · Bioko
Greenville · Sassandra · Grand Bassam · Winneba · Oktika · Kumba · Limbé
C. Palmas · Tabou · San-Pédro · Abidjan · Axim · C. Three Points · Rey Malabo

1 : 20 000 000

MEDITERRANEAN SEA

TURKEY
Antalya Aleppo Mosul
CYPRUS Latakia SYRIA Mesopotamia
Nicosia Hama Homs
Iraklion Crete Rhodes Limassol Tripoli
LEBANON Beirut Damascus IRAQ
Akko Haifa Al Rutbah
ISRAEL Tel Aviv-Jaffa Jerusalem Amman
Rashid Damietta Gaza Khan Yunis Dead Sea JORDAN
Alexandria Mansûra Port Said Be'er Sheva Ma'ân
Damanhûr Tanta El 'Arîsh Al Jawf
CAIRO Zagazig Ismailia Elat Al Aqabah
El Giza Helwân Suez Nafud Desert
Qâra Sinai Pen. Tabûk SAUDI
Qattâra Depression El Faiyûm Beni Suef Al Muwaylih Taymâ'
Sîwa Arabian Madâ'in Salih
El Bawîti Beni Mazâr ARABIA
El Minya Desert Al Wajh
Mallawi Dairût Bûr Safâga
Qasr Farâfra Asyût Abu Tig Quseir Umm Lajj
Sohâg Akhmîm Qena Medina
El Wâhat el-Dakhla El Qasr Girga Luxor Qûs Yanbu'al Bahr
Mût El Khârga Isna Idfu
El Wâhat el-Khârga Bârîs Aswân Umm Lajj
Dunqu Aswân High Dam El Shallal Rabigh Qasr
Lake Nasser Bîr Shalatein Jedda At Tâ'if
Bîr Ungat Halaib Mecca Al Lith

LIBYA Cyrenaica Libyan Desert EGYPT RED SEA
Tripoli (Tarabulus) Al Khums Zlitan Misrâtah
Al Qasabât Gharyân Banîn Al Bayda Darnah
968 Banî Walîd Benghazi Suluq 878 Tubruq Ras al Milh
Mizdah Al Bu'ayrât Surt Marsa el Brega Al 'Uqaylah Sîdi Barrâni
Tripolitania G. of Sidra Az Zuwaytinah Ajdabiyah Salûm Marsâ Matrûh El Alamein
Adrî Brach Al Jaghbûb Al Alamein Damanhûr
Sabhah Zillah Hûn Marâdah Awjilah
Awbârî Fezzan 1200 Zillah Ma'tan as Sarra
Tasâwah Marzûq Tmassah Al Jazirah Rebiana Al Jawf Kufra Oasis
Wâw al Kabîr Al Qatrûn Tropic of Cancer
Madama 3150 Tarso Emissi Toummo Aozou Bardai Ma'ten as Sarra
Djado Wour Zouar I'Uweinat 1893 Ayn al 'Uwaynat El Wâhat el Selîma Wadi Halfa
Chirfa Tibesti Emi Koussi 3415 Gouri Kosha Abri Nubian Desert
Anaye Ouninga-Kébir Ounianga Sérir Laqiya Arba'in Delgo 2635 Port Sudan
Bilma Faya-Largeau Fada Nukheila 3rd Cataract Argo Abu Hamed Suakin
Oum Chalouba Bir 'Atrun Dongola El Kab Sinkat Trinkitat
L. Chad Zigey Arada Biltine El Khandaq Kareima 4th Cataract 5th Cataract Haiya Junction Tokar
Nguigmi Rig-Rig Mao Kutum Merowe Berber Musmar Derudub
Massakory Yao L. Fitri Abéché Adré Al Junaynah Kabkabîyah El Fâsher Korti Atbara Adorama Karora
Ndjamena Oum Hadjer Am Dam Goz Beïda Ed Debba Ed Dâmer
Massaguet Bitkine Mongo Zalingei Umm Keddada Umm Bel Wad Hamid Shendî Nakfa
Maroua CHAD Massénya Hajar Banga Nyala 3088 J. Marrah Wad Banda 6th Cataract Geili ERITREA Keren Mitsiwa
Mgalala Chari Melfi Abou-Deïa Idd al Ghanam Taweisha En Nahud Abû Zabad Omdurmân El Khartûm Bahrî Kassala Akordat Asmera Zula
Kélo Bongor Bousso Mongororo Rahad al Bardî Buram El Odaiya Umm Ruwaba Khartoum Kâmlin Khashm el Girba Barentu Adi Ugri
Lère Gounou-Gaya Kyabé Birao Songo Muglad El Laqawa El Obeid Er Rahad Rufa'a Wâd Medanî Gedaref 4620 Ras Dashen Mekele
Moundou Doba Am-Timan Manguéigne Abu Matariq Heiban Dilling Rashad Ed Dueim Sennâr Gallâbât Metema Gonder Sekota
Goré Moïssala Ndélé Daïm Zubeir Kâdugli Talodi Kaka Ellebelein El Mafâza L. Tana Debre Tabor Mekdela
CENTRAL AFRICAN REPUBLIC Ouanda Djallé Kafia Kingi Raga Tungaru Kodok Melut Er Roseires Karmuk Abbay Dembecha Mota
Kaga Bandoro Batangafo Markounda Bria Yalinga Bentiu Malakâl Abwong Renk Famaka Alibo Debre Markos
Bossangoa Bakala Ippy Djema Obo White Nile Fangak Sobat Nasir Gambela ETHIOPIA Addis Ababa Addis Alem
Bossemptélé Bouca Grimari Bambari Bakouma Gogrial Tur Bahr el Ghazal Duk Faiwil Akôbo Gore Dembidolo Gimbi
Bozoum Sibut Bangassou Zémio Amadi Tali P. Tombe Majî Omo Jima L. Shala Asela
Bouar Carnot Boali Bangui Mobaye Bomu ZAÏRE Yakoma Bondo Dungu Faradje Mongalla Jûba Chencha L. Abaya 4200 L. Shamo Gidole Jarso Burji
Bertoua Batouri Berbérati Bambio Uele Aba Kaya Kaji Tarit KENYA Lokitaung L. Turkana Chew Bahir Mega Arero

COPYRIGHT. GEORGE PHILIP & SON. LTD

1 : 8 000 000

50   0   50   100   150   200 miles
50   0   100   200   300 km

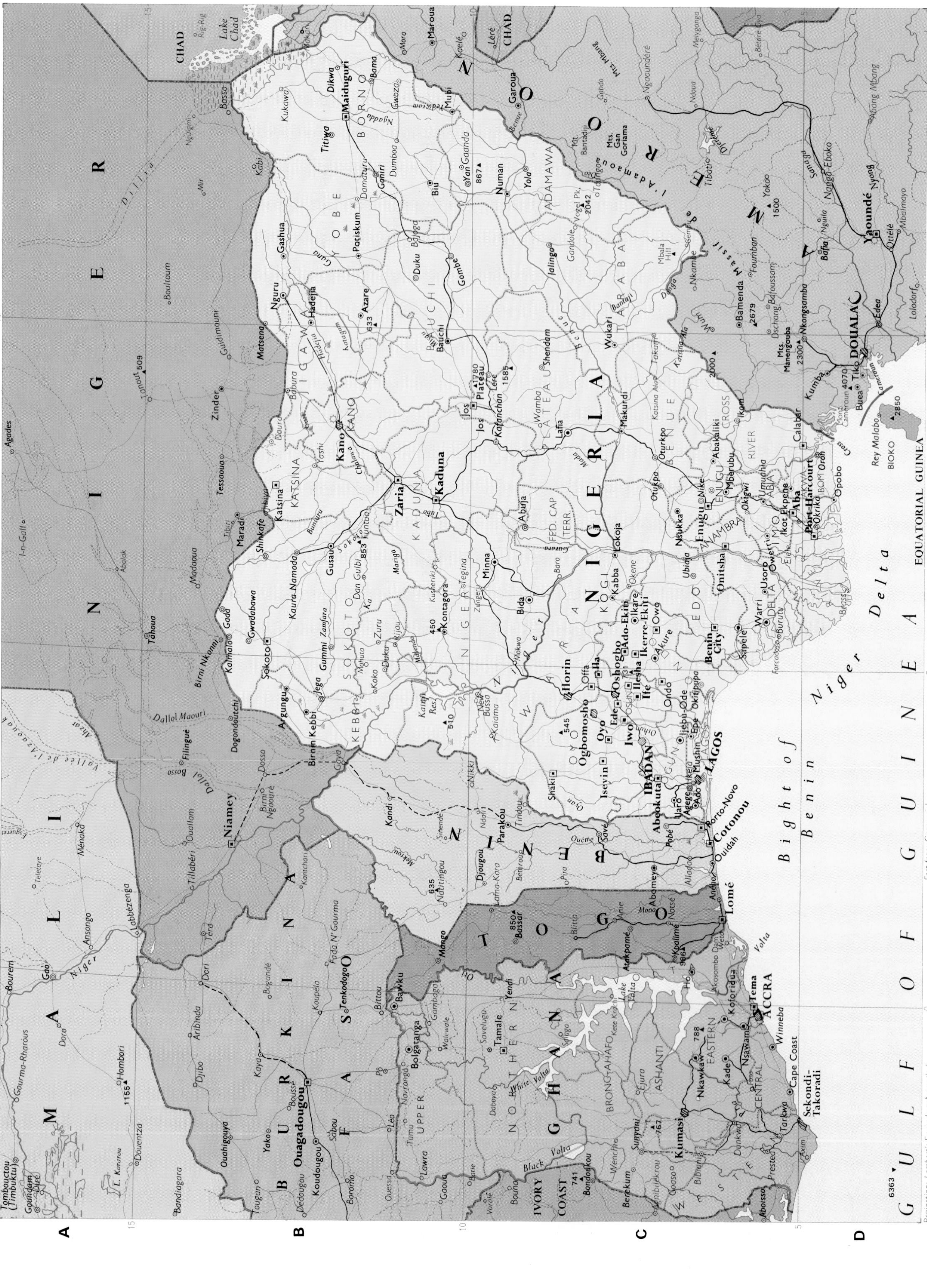

COPYRIGHT. GEORGE PHILIP LTD

CHAD
Lake Chad
Rig-Rig

NIGER

MALI

BURKINA FASO

CAMEROUN

NIGERIA

BENIN

TOGO

GHANA

IVORY COAST

EQUATORIAL GUINEA

GULF OF GUINEA

Bight of Benin

Niger Delta

BORNO

YOBE

JIGAWA

KANO

KATSINA

SOKOTO

KEBBI

ZAMFARA

KADUNA

BAUCHI

PLATEAU

ADAMAWA

TARABA

GONGOLA

BENUE

NIGER

KWARA

KOGI

OYO

OSUN

ONDO

EDO

DELTA

ANAMBRA

ENUGU

ABIA

IMO

RIVER

CROSS RIVER

LAGOS

FED. CAP. TERR.

Abuja

LAGOS
IBADAN
ACCRA
DOUALA
Yaoundé
Niamey
Ouagadougou
Kano
Kaduna
Zaria
Port-Harcourt
Maiduguri
Lomé
Cotonou
Porto-Novo
Benin City
Ilorin
Ogbomosho
Oshogbo
Ife
Abeokuta
Ado-Ekiti
Akure
Onitsha
Enugu
Calabar
Sokoto
Gusau
Katsina
Maradi
Zinder
Tahoua
Agades
Gashua
Nguru
Hadejia
Azare
Bauchi
Jos
Gombe
Yola
Numan
Jalingo
Makurdi
Wukari
Lafia
Minna
Kontagora
Bida
Lokoja
Kabba
Warri
Sapele
Oyo
Iwo
Ilesha
Ede
Eps
Ijebu-Ode
Kumasi
Tamale
Tema
Cape Coast
Sekondi-Takoradi
Winneba
Nsawam
Koforidua
Ho
Kpandu
Bolgatanga
Bawku
Yendi
Salaga
Wa
Mango
Sokodé
Atakpamé
Kpalimé
Anloga
Parakou
Kandi
Natitingou
Djougou
Ouidah
Allada
Save
Abomey

NORTHERN
ASHANTI
EASTERN
CENTRAL
WESTERN
BRONG-AHAFO
VOLTA

Lake Volta
White Volta
Black Volta
Niger
Benue
Volta
Mono
Oueme

Bioko
Rey Malabo
2850
Buea 4070
Mt. Cameroun

Tombouctou (Timbuktu)
Gao
Timbuktu

East from Greenwich
Projection: Lambert's Equivalent Azimuthal

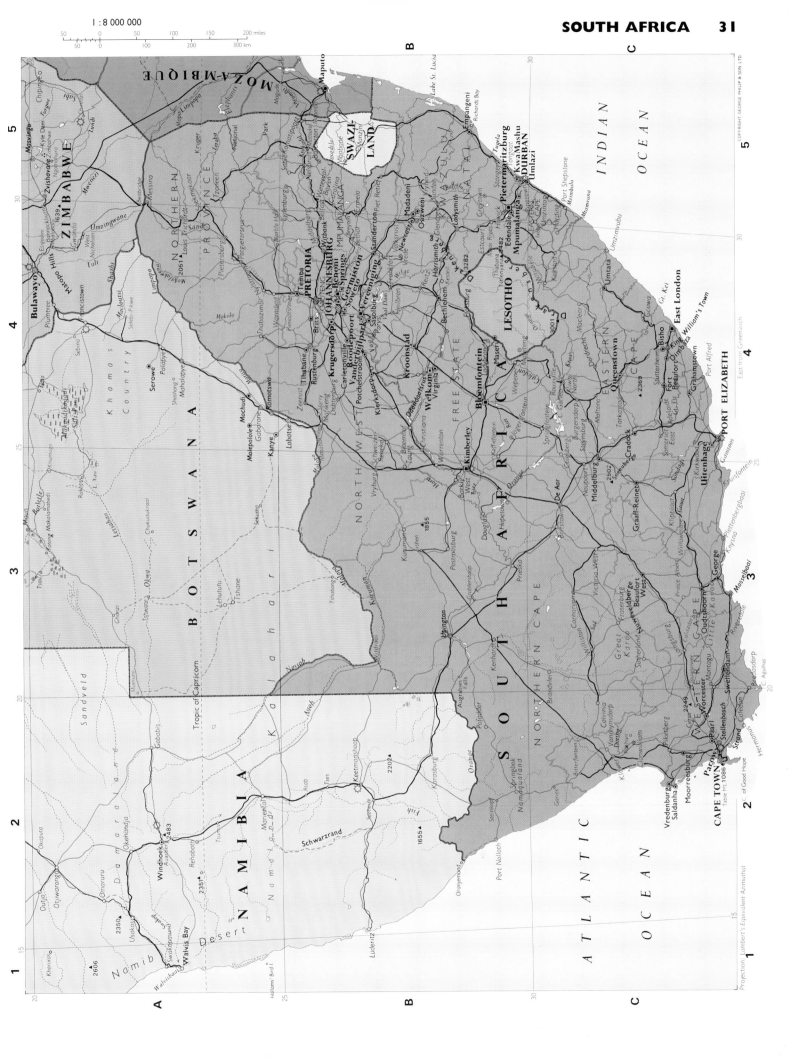

1 : 8 000 000

50   0   50   100   150   200 miles
50   0   100   200   300 km

MOZAMBIQUE

ZIMBABWE

Bulawayo

NAMIBIA

BOTSWANA

Windhoek

Walvis Bay

SOUTH AFRICA

NORTHERN PROVINCE

Pretoria

JOHANNESBURG

MPUMALANGA

SWAZILAND

KWAZULU NATAL

Durban

Pietermaritzburg

LESOTHO

Maseru

FREE STATE

Bloemfontein

Kimberley

NORTH WEST

NORTHERN CAPE

EASTERN CAPE

WESTERN CAPE

Port Elizabeth

East London

CAPE TOWN

INDIAN OCEAN

ATLANTIC OCEAN

Tropic of Capricorn

Namib Desert

Kalahari

Projection: Lambert's Equivalent Azimuthal

East from Greenwich

COPYRIGHT GEORGE PHILIP & SON, LTD.

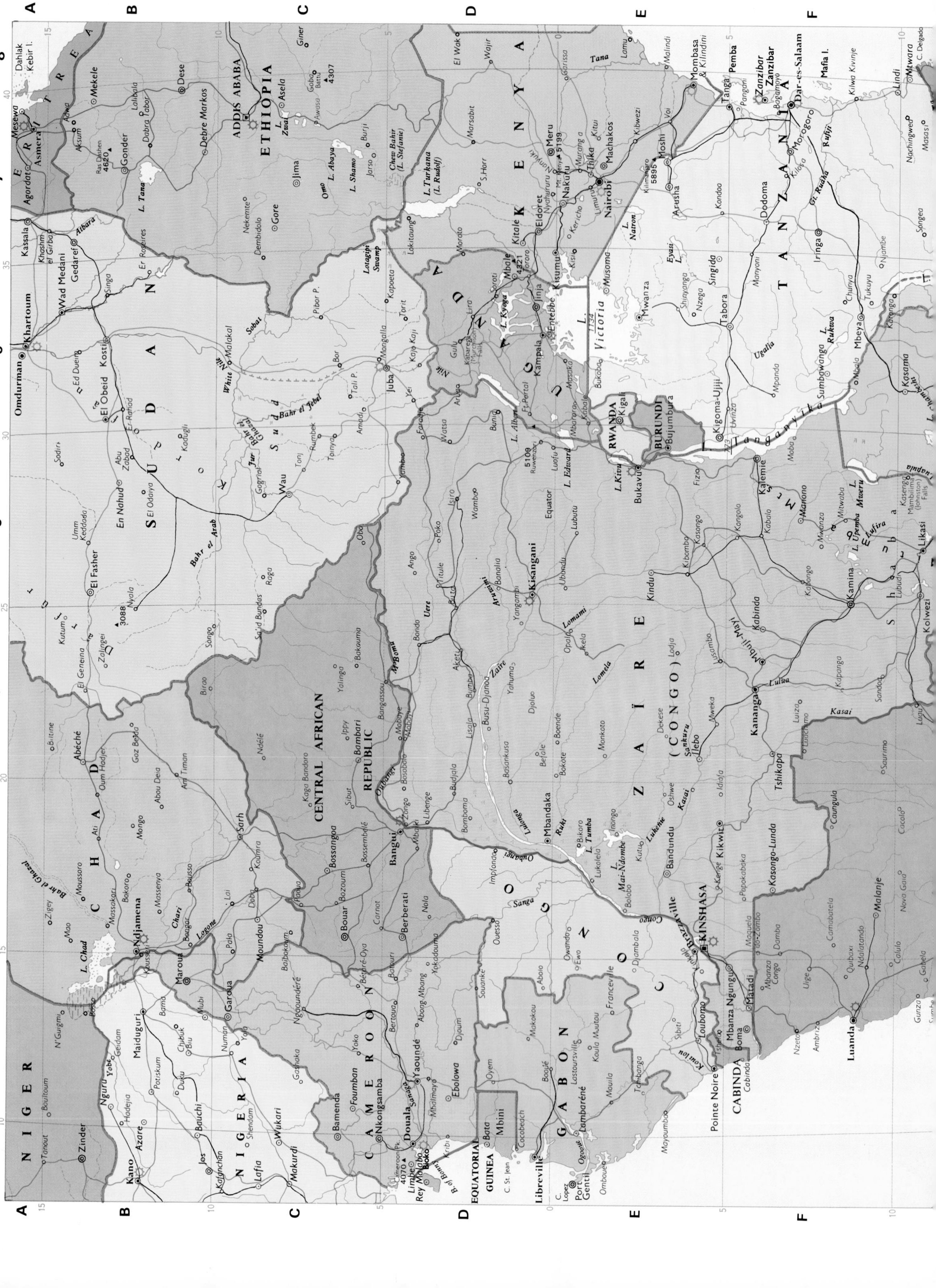

ERITREA

Dahlak Kebir I.

Mesewa
Asmera
Agordat
Keren
Mekele
Lalibela
Debre Markos
Dese
Debre Tabor
Gonder
ADDIS ABABA
ETHIOPIA
Aksum
Ras Dashen 4620
L. Tana
Nekemte
Gore
Dembidolo
Jima
Omo
L. Abaya
L. Shamo
Giner
Gobo Bottu 4307
Awassa Asela
L. Zeuai
Burji
Chew Bahir (L. Stefanie)
Jarso

Kassala
Khashm el Girba
Gedaref
Singa
Er Roseires
Wad Medani
Khartoum
Omdurman
Ed Dueim
El Obeid
Er Rahad
Kosti

S U D A N

Sobat
Malakal
White Nile
Bahr el Jebel
Bahr el Ghazal

Marsabit
L. Turkana (L. Rudolf)
Lokitaung
Lodwar
S. Horr

K E N Y A
El Wak
Wajir
Tana
Garissa
Meru
Mt Kenya 5199
Nanyuki
Eldoret
Kitale
Mbale
Tororo
Kisumu
Nakuru
Nairobi
Thika
Machakos
Murang'a
Nyahururu
Kericho
Kisii
Musoma

Mombasa & Kilindini
Malindi
Tanga
Pemba
Zanzibar
Dar-es-Salaam
Mafia I.
Kilwa Kivinje
Lindi
C. Delgado
Mtwara
Nachingwea

Kiloga
Moshi
Arusha
Kondoa
Dodoma
T A N Z A N I A
Eyasi L.
Singida
Shinyanga
Nzega
Tabora
Iringa
Mbeya
Kasama

Mwanza
Lake Victoria
Bukoba
Entebbe
Kampala
Jinja

U G A N D A
Gulu
Juba
Torit
Yei

RWANDA
Kigali
BURUNDI
Bujumbura
Bukavu
Goma
L. Kivu
L. Edward
L. Albert
Ruwenzori 5109
L. Tanganyika
Kigoma-Ujiji
Kalemie
Kabalo
Kongolo
Kamina
Kindu

Z A I R E (C O N G O)
Kisangani
Kananga
Mbuji-Mayi
Kolwezi
Kabinda
Lodja
Ilebo
Kikwit
Bandundu
Mbandaka
KINSHASA
Brazzaville

C A M E R O O N
Ndjamena
C H A D
L. Chad
Maiduguri

N I G E R I A
N I G E R
Zinder
Kano

CENTRAL AFRICAN REPUBLIC
Bangui
Bangassou
Bambari
Berberati
Bouar
Bossangoa

G A B O N
Libreville
Port Gentil
EQUATORIAL GUINEA
Bata
Mbini
Yaoundé
Douala

C O N G O
Pointe Noire
Loubomo
CABINDA
Matadi
Boma
Luanda

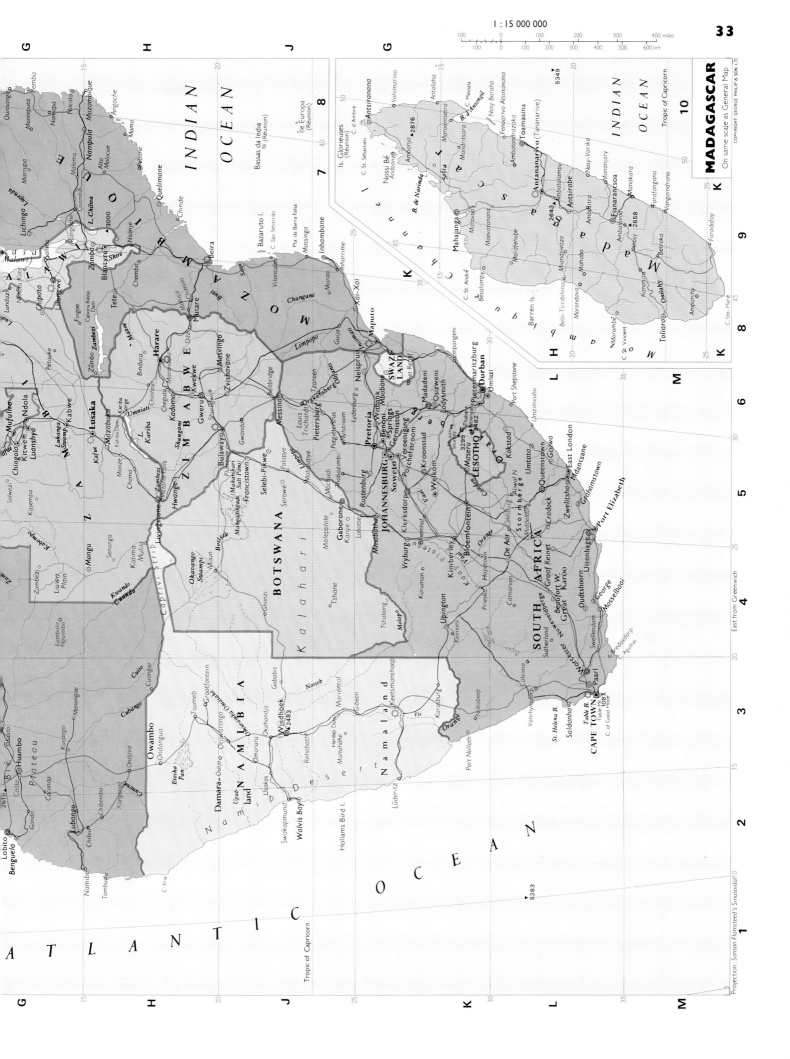

1 : 15 000 000

100   0   100   200   300   400 miles
100   0   100   200   300   400   500   600 km

COPYRIGHT GEORGE PHILIP & SON LTD

MADAGASCAR
On same scale as General Map

INDIAN   OCEAN

Tropic of Capricorn

INDIAN
OCEAN

Is. Glorieuses (Réunion)
C. d'Ambre
Antsiranana   Vohimarina
C. St. Sébastien   Antalaha
2876   B. d'Antomal   Nosy Boraha
Nossi Bé   Maroantsetra
Andoany   Mandritsara
B. de Narinda   Sofia   Fenoarivo Atsinanana
Mahajanga   Maevatanana   Toamasina
Moevatonana
AntananarIvo (Tananarive)
C. St. André   Ambatolampy
2643   Antsirabe
Besalampy   Ambositra
Barren Is.   Miandrivazo   Manjary
5349   Mandgovazo   Mananjary
Morombe   Ambalavao   Manakara
N. Morombe   2658   Farafangana
C. St. Vincent   Fianarantsoa   Vangaindrano
Betroka
Morondava
Belo-Tsiribihina   Kanohira
Toliaro   Ampanihy
Onilahy   Betroka
Faradofay
C. Ste. Marie

INDIAN   OCEAN

Quissanga
Pemba
Montepuez   Namapa
Marrupa   Nacala
Lichinga   Namuno   Mozambique
L. Chilwa   Nampula   Angoche
Alto Molocue
Gurue   Moma
Sofrie   Mozambique
3000   Namacurra
Zomba   Quelimane
Blantyre   Shire
MALAWI (Nyasa)   Nsanje
ASSA   Morrumbala   Chinde
(Malawi)   Mocuba   Ile Europa (Réunion)
Salima   Bassas da India
Lilongwe   Beira
Chipota
Chromo   C. São Sebastião
Cabora Bassa   Bazaruto I.
Dam   Vilanculos   Pta da Barra Falsa
Tete   Chemba   Mossoro
Mangochi   Changane   Inhambane
Zombo Zumbo Zambezi   Inharrime
Fingoe   Mutare
Petauke   Bindura   Odzi   Xai-Xai
HARARE   Marondera   Chokwe
Mazoe   Guija   Maputo
ZIMBABWE   Limpopo   SWAZI
Gweru   Masvingo   LAND
Bulawayo   Zvishavane   Nelspruit
Kwekwe   Beitbridge   Madadeni
Shurugwi   Messina   Osizweni   Pietermaritzburg
Gwanda   Louis   Ladysmith   Durban
Plumtree   Trichardt   Umlazi
Francistown   Pietersburg   Port Shepstone
Selebi-Pikwe   Potgietersrus   Thabana N
Palapye   Lydenburg   3482   Umzimkulu
Serowe   Nylstroom   LESOTHO
Mahalapye   Witbank   Maseru
Mochudi   PRETORIA   3299   Kokstad
Molepolole   Benoni   Umtata
GABORONE   Springs   Kroonstad   Queenstown   Mdantsane
Kanye   Germiston   Welkom   East London
Lobatse   JOHANNESBURG   Stormberge   Cradock
Soweto   Klerksdorp   Middelburg   Zwelitsha
Ramatlhabama   Vereeniging   De Aar   Grahamstown
Mmabatho   Klerksdorp   Bloemfontein   Uitenhage
Vryburg   Aliwal N   Port Elizabeth
Kuruman   Kimberley   SOUTH   George
Upington   Hopetown   AFRICA   Mosselbaai
Keimoes   Carnarvon   Graaff Reinet   Oudtshoorn
Kenhardt   Beaufort W   Swellendam
Prieska   Great   Worcester
Kakamas   Sutherland   Karoo   Paarl
Calvinia   Niewoudtville   CAPE TOWN
Pofadder   Table Mt   C. of Good Hope
Springbok   108   Agulhas
Port Nolloth   Saldanha   Bredasdorp
St. Helena B.   C. of Good Hope

NAMIBIA   BOTSWANA
Grootfontein   Kalahari
Tsumeb   (Makarikari)
Otavi   Makgadikgadi Salt Pans
Otjiwarongo   Ghanzi
Omaruru   Tshane
WINDHOEK   Tshabong
2483   Molopo
Rehoboth   Nossob
Gobabis   Gobobs
Mariental   Vis
Keetmanshoop   Orange
Gibeon
Bethanie   Karasburg
Namaland
Lüderitz   Noordoewer
Karasburg   Port Nolloth
Orange

ZAMBIA
Lubumbashi   Mufulira
Chingola   Ndola
Kitwe   Kabwe
Luanshya   LUSAKA
Lukanga
Swamp   Kafue
Kariba
L.   Dam
Kariba   Kariba Gorge
Mongu   Victoria Falls
Senanga   Livingstone
Katima Mulilo   Hwange
Kwando   Caprivi Strip
Sesheke

ANGOLA
Lobito   Kito
Benguela   Huambo
Namibe   Cuima
Tombua   Conda
C. Fria   Chibemba
Chibia   Matala
Lubango   Cassinga
Chinamacondo
Owambo   Oshikango
Ondangua   Ondjiva
Ovamboland
Eiseb Pan   Runtu
Okavango   Rundu
Swamps
Okavango Swamps

ATLANTIC   OCEAN

5283

Tropic of Capricorn

Projection: Sanson Flamsteed's Sinusoidal

East from Greenwich

INDONESIA

Sulawesi (Celebes)
Kendari
Butung
Ujung Pandang (Makasar)
Buru
Ceram
Ambon
Misool
Fakfak
Sorong
Vogelkop
Pegunungan Maoke
Puncak Jaya 5020
Irian Jaya
Jayapura
Biak
Sumbawa
Flores
Flores Sea
Ende
Robo
Kupang
Wetar
Alor
Leti
Babar
Dili
3310
Timor
Timor Sea
Sumba
6204
Banda Sea
5300
7260
Kai Is.
3350
Aru Is.
Tanimbar Is.
Pulau Yos Sudarso
Arafura Sea

PAPUA NEW GUINEA
Bismarck Archipelago
Wewak
Madang
Mount Hagen
4508 Mt. Wilhelm
Lae
New Guinea
Fly
Owen Stanley Range
Gulf of Papua
Port Moresby
Torres Strait
New Ireland
Kavieng
150
New Britain
Rabaul
Solomon Sea
D'Entrecaste
Louisiade Archipelago

Coral
Coral Sea
Islan
Territo

C. York
Weipa
Cape York
Cape York Peninsula
C. Croker
C. Arnhem
Melville I.
Darwin
Arnhem Land
Gulf of Carpentaria
Wellesley I.
Cooktown
Cairns
1611 Bartle Frere
Normanton
Forsayth
Townsville
Charters Towers
Mackay

C. Londonderry
Cambridge G.
Wyndham
Kimberley Plateau
Derby
Broome
Daly Waters
Larrimah
Barkly Tableland
NORTHERN
Tanami Desert
Tennant Creek
Mitchell
Flinders
Kajaabi
Mount Isa
Hughenden
Winton
QUEENSLAND
Longreach
Rockhampton
Gladstone
Bundc

Great Sandy Desert
L. Mackay
TERRITORY
Macdonnell Ranges
1510 Mt. Ziel
Alice Springs
AUSTRALIA
Diamantina
Yaraka
Maryborough
Gympie

Dampier
Port Hedland
N.W. Cape
Mt. Bruce 1226
Hamersley Range
Newman
Lake Disappointment
Gibson Desert
Simpson Desert
Ayers Rock
Mt. Woodroffe 1440
Musgrave Ranges
SOUTH
Cooper Creek
Lake Eyre
Grey Range
Charleville
Roma
Quilpie
Cunnamulla
Thargomindah
Dirrabandi
BRISBANE
Toowoomba

WESTERN
L. Carnegie
Great Victoria Desert
AUSTRALIA
Leonora
Carnarvon
Meekatharra
Marree
Flinders Range
Bourke
Walgett
NEW SOUTH
Tamworth
Round Mt. 1616
Tare

Geraldton
Lake Barlee
Leonora
Kalgoorlie-Boulder
Tarcoola
Deakin
Nullarbor Plain
Penong
Port Augusta
Port Pirie
Whyalla
Broken Hill
Darling
Cobar
WALES
Orange
Dubbo
Bathurst
Newcastle
SYDNE
Wollong
Shellharbou

Murchison
Northam
Norseman
Great Australian Bight
5632
Spencer Gulf
Adelaide
Murray
Mildura
Wagga Wagga
Canberra
CAPITAL TERRITORY
Perth
Bunbury
Esperance
Port Lincoln
Kangaroo I.
Encounter B.
Shepparton
Albury
Murray
Mt. Kosciusko 2237
Australian Alps
Bombala
C. Howe

Darling Range
C. Leeuwin
Augusta
Albany
Horsham
Bendigo
VICTORIA
Australian
Ballarat
MELBOURNE
Geelong
Mount Gambier
Warrnambool
Bass Strait
King I.
Furneaux Group

INDIAN OCEAN

TASMANIA
Burnie
Launceston
1617 Mt. Ossa
Hobart
S.E. Cape

1 : 20 000 000

100   0   100   200   300   400 miles
100   0   100   200   300   400   500   600 km

10   11   12   13   14   16

M   Tamana   *K*   Baker   Equator
e   170
NAURU   I   R   I   B   A   T   I
l   ▾ 6195
Bougainville *a*   A
Choiseul *n*   Namumea   Abariringa
SOLOMON *e* Santa Isabel   Phoenix Is.
New *s* ISLANDS   Carondelet
Georgia *i*   5
Honiara ▲ 2331 *a*   TUVALU
Guadalcanal   San   (Ellice Is.) Funafuti ○Funafuti
          Cristóbal   Nukulaelae
h.   Santa Cruz Is.   B
Rennell   ▾ 7223   Tokelau
                   Fataka   Is.
e a   Rotuma   (N.Z.)
                                                      10
                Banks Is.   Mata-Utu○Uvea WESTERN
          Espíritu Santo ▲1880 VANUATU Wallis & Futuna SAMOA
                Malakula   (New Hebrides) Horn (Fr.) Savai'i Apia
Chesterfield Is.   Port-Vila○Efate   Upolu○ C
                                          Vanua Levu   Niuafo'ou   Tutuila
                                     Viti Levu   American
                                          7324○ FIJI   Samoa
                                     New   Suva   Lau Is.   15
                ▲1628 Loyalty Is.   Vavau Is.
          New   ▾7569   TONGA
          Caledonia   Ha'apai Is.
          (Fr.) Nouméa   ○Niue
                               Ceve-i-Ra   Nuku'Alofa○   (N.Z.)   D
              Matthew   Tongatapu Is.
     P   A   C   I   F   I   C   Tonga Trench   Cook Is.
                                     10 882▾   (N.Z.)   20
                5303   Tropic of Capricorn
          O   C   E   A   N   E
                                                                25
                Norfolk
                (Austr.)
                               Raoul   F
     Lord Howe   Kermadec Is.
     (Austr.)   (N.Z.)
          ▾ 734   30
                                     10 047▾ Kermadec Trench
a s m a n   S e a   North C.   International Date Line
                Kaitaia ○   G
                     Whangarei
          Auckland ○   North Island
          Hamilton ○   Bay of Plenty
              New Plymouth○ Rotorua
          NEW   ○Raupehu Gisborne   35
          ZEALAND   2797 ○Napier
              Wanganui○ Palmerston
              Nelson○ North
          South Island Blenheim○Wellington
              Greymouth○ Cook Strait   H
                Mt.Cook Southern Alps
          ▾ 5267 3753 ○Christchurch
                ○Timaru
              Wakatipu   40
          Invercargill○ ○Dunedin   Chatham
                Stewart   (N.Z.)   J

10   11   12   13   14   15   16   17   18

COPYRIGHT. GEORGE PHILIP LTD.

Projection: Mollweide's Homolographic
East from Greenwich

ALASKA

Gulf of Alaska
Prince of Wales I.
Queen Charlotte Is.
Juneau
Kitimat
Prince Rupert

▲5959

GREENLAND   C. Farewell

Hudson Bay

C A N A D A

N O R T H   A M E R I C A

N O R T H

Edmonton
Vancouver
Vancouver I.
Victoria
Seattle
Portland

Calgary   Regina   Winnipeg
L. Winnipeg

L. Superior
Minneapolis
CHICAGO
Boise
Snake

Montréal   Quebec
Ottawa   Saint John
Toronto   L. Ontario
Detroit   Buffalo   Boston   C. Sable
Pittsburgh
Cincinnati

Labrador

Newfoundland
Pr. Edward I.

St. Lawrence

L. Huron
L. Erie
Michigan

NEW YORK
Philadelphia
Baltimore
Washington

A T L A N T I C

C. Mendocino
San Francisco

Rocky Mountains

Salt Lake City
Denver   Kansas
St. Louis

▲4418

U N I T E D   S T A T E S
Oklahoma

Memphis   Atlanta
Mississippi

Appalachian Mts.

C. Hatteras

Bermuda (U.K.)

O C E A N

▼6741

Los Angeles
San Diego

Dallas

Ciudad Juarez

Sierra Madre
M E X I C O
Gulf of California

San Antonio
Houston

Jacksonville
New Orleans

Miami
Gulf of Mexico

Florida Strait
Havana
CUBA

BAHAMAS

Hawaiian Is.
(U.S.)
Honolulu   Oahu

Tropic of Cancer

6225 ▼

Monterrey

▲6225

West Indies

Ridge

Hawaii

Revilla Gigedo Is.
(Mexico)

Guadalajara
Puebla   México
5700
Acapulco

Yucatan Channel
Mérida

BELIZE

▼7680
JAMAICA
Kingston

Hispaniola   9200
DOM.
REP.
HAITI
PUERTO
RICO

Leeward
Is.

I F I C

on I. (U.S.)

GUATEMALA
Guatemala
Salvador
EL SALVADOR
CENTRAL
AMERICA
HONDURAS

NICARAGUA
Managua

Caribbean Sea

BARBADOS
Windward
Is. TRINIDAD &
TOBAGO

Palmyra Is. (U.S.)
Teraina
Tabuaeran
Kiritimati

COSTA RICA
San José
PANAMA
Panama Canal

Barranquilla

San
Orinoco

Maracaibo

Caracas

VENEZUELA

Clipperton I. (Fr.)

Cocos I.

Medellín
Bogota
Cali
COLOMBIA

G

Jarvis I.
(U.S.)

E A N

Equator

Galápagos
(Ecuador)

Guayaquil
Quito
ECUADOR
Iquitos

Manaus
Amazon

ry I.
ix Is.
Malden I.
Starbuck I.

B A T I

C. Pariñas

BRAZIL
SOUTH

Marquesas Is.

Trujillo

Tongareva
Penrhyn Is.
Manihiki
Suwarrow Is.

Caroline I.

Vostok
I.
Flint I.

6369 ▼

PERU
Lima
Cuzco

AMERICA

L. Titicaca
Illampu & Ancohuma
6550
La Paz
BOLIVIA

Cook
Islands
(N.Z.)

Society Is.
Windward
Is.
Tahiti
Manuae

Leeward Is.

Tuamotu
Archipelago

FRENCH POLYNESIA

Arequipa

▼6866

Peru–

Antofagasta
Trench
8050 ▼

PARAGUAY

Asunción

Austral

Rarotonga

Seamount Chain

Mururoa

Tropic of Capricorn

Tubuai Is.
(Austral Is.)

Rapa Iti

Pitcairn I. (U.K.)

Ducie I
(U.K.)

Sala-y-Gomez
(Chile)

Easter Is.
(Chile)

San Félix (Chile)

San Ambrosio (Chile)

Iquique
Chile

Tucumán

Pto. Alegre

URUGUAY

Arch. de Juan Fernández
(Chile)

▼6960

Córdoba
Rosario

Valparaíso
Santiago

Buenos Aires
Montevideo

Río de la Plata

Andes

Concepción

A R G E N T I N A

SOUTH

Pacific – Antarctic Ridge

East Pacific Ridge

Tuamotu Ridge

Christmas Island Ridge

Chile Rise

Chonos Arch.

Patagonia

ATLANTIC

G. of Penas

▼6212

OCEAN

Punta Arenas
Str. of Magellan
Tierra del Fuego
C. Horn

Falkland Is. (U.K.)

South Georgia

West from Greenwich

COPYRIGHT. GEORGE PHILIP & SON. LTD.

ALASKA

1:30 000 000

0   200   400   600 km

Projection: Bonne

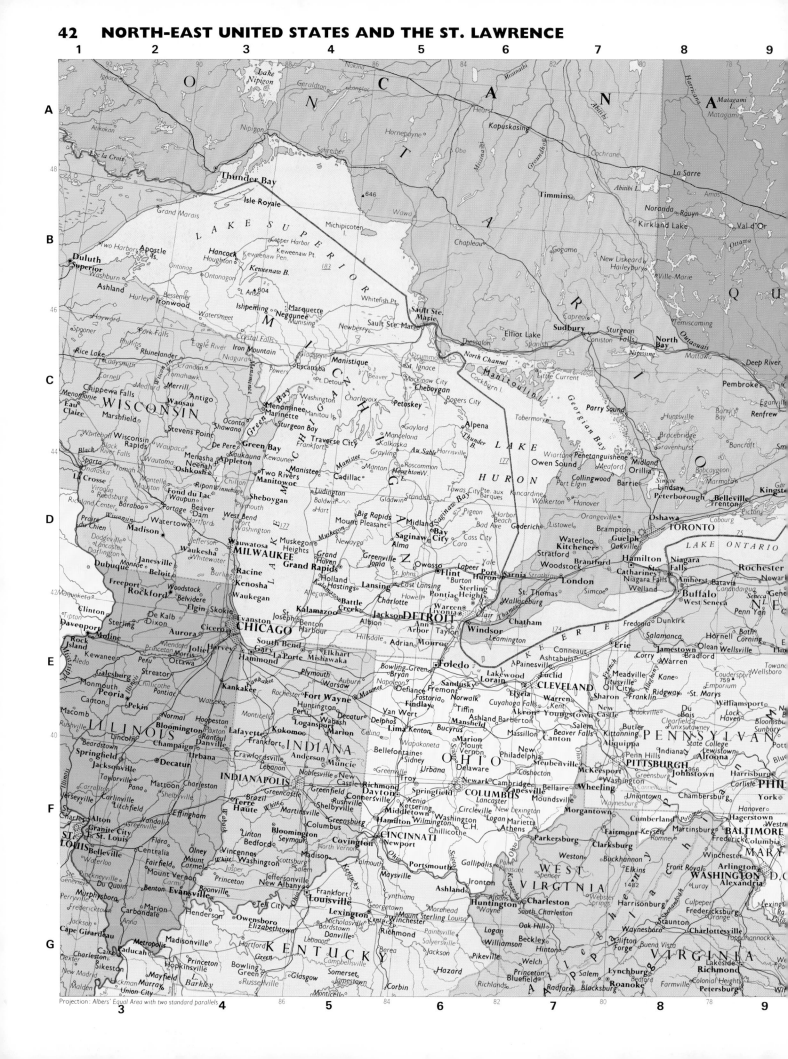

Projection: Albers' Equal Area with two standard parallels

1 : 6 000 000

50   50   100   150 miles
50   0   50   100   150   200
km

A

B

C

D

E

F

G

D   **A**
556 ▲
Chibougamau
Chibougamau L.
Pipmuacan L.
Port-Cartier
West Pt.
Anticosti I.
Jupiter
Heath Pt.

Peribonca
Cap-Chat
Matane
Shickshock Mts.
Gaspé Peninsula
1310
C. Gaspé
Gaspé
▼ 572
GULF OF
ST. LAWRENCE

Dolbeau
Gouin
Res.
St. Félicien
Lac
St. Jean
Roberval
Chicoutimi
Saguenay
Jonquière
St. Lawrence
Rimouski
Rivière du Loup
Campbellton
Dalhousie
Chaleur Bay
Bathurst
Miramichi B.
North Pt.
Tignish
Magdalen
Is.
(Quebec)
C. North

Gatineau
B   **E**   **C**
L'Annonciation
Res.
Baskatong
La Tuque
Baie St. Paul
Edmundston
Fort
Kent Van
Buren
Grand
Falls
N   **E**   **W**
819 ▲
Newcastle
Chatham
Northumberland Str.
Summerside
PRINCE EDWARD
ISLAND
East Pt.
Charlottetown
Cape Breton
532 ▲
Island
Glace Bay
Sydney

968 ▲
Grand-Mère
Shawinigan
Cap-de-la-Madeleine
Trois-Rivières
Louiseville
Quebec
Île d'Orléans
Lauzon
Lévis
Montmagny
Ste-Marie
Eagle
Lake
Caribou
St. John
Allagash
B   **R**   **U**   **N**   **S**   **W**   **I**   **C**   **K**
Chipman
Grand L.
Moncton
Springhill
Stellarton
New Glasgow
Bras d'Or
L.
Chedabucto B.
Canso

Joliette
St-
Jérôme
Victoriaville
Plessisville
St-George
Thetford
Mines
Eagle L.
Chamberlain
L.
Chesuncook
1605 ▲
Mt Katahdin
Patten
Houlton
Fredericton
Grand L.
N   **O**   **V**   **A**
Truro
Dartmouth

Hawkesbury
Ottawa
St-
Hyacinthe
Sorel
Drummondville
Asbestos
Moosehead
L.
Millinocket
Chiputneticook
Lakes
Saint
John
Sussex
S   **C**   **O**   **T**   **I**   **A**
Kentville
Halifax

Cornwall
St-Jean
Beauharnois
MONTREAL
Lachine
Granby
Sherbrooke
Magog
Coaticook
Lac-
Mégantic
Greenville
Mattawamkeag
Lincoln
St. Stephen
Calais
St. Stephen
Bay of Fundy
Digby
Bridgewater

Malone
Massena
Plattsburgh
Newport
St. Albans
Cowansville
Richardson
Lakes
Dover
Foxcroft
Old Town
M   **A**   **I**   **N**   **E**
East-
port
Grand
Manan I.
Rossignol Res.
Shelburne
C. Sable

Ogdensburg
Potsdam
Canton
Champlain
L.
Burlington
Winooski
Island Pond
Lancaster
Berlin
Farmington
Skowhegan
Bangor
Brewer
Machias
Yarmouth

Watertown
Lowville
Saranac Lakes
Gouverneur
1629 ▲
Adirondack Mts.
Ticonderoga
L.
VERMONT
Montpelier
Barre
Johnsbury
Rumford
Augusta
Waterville
Gardiner
Belfast
Ellsworth
Bar
Harbor
Mt. Desert
Grand
L.

Rome
Utica
Gloversville
Amsterdam
Lake Pleasant
Middlebury
Rutland
Lebanon
Claremont
Mt
Washington
1917
Auburn
Lewiston
Rockland
Penobscot B.

Syracuse
Schenectady
Oneida L.
Granville
Springfield
Glens
Falls
Saratoga Springs
Hudson
Falls
Keene
Concord
White
Mts.
NEW HAMPSHIRE
Conway
Brunswick
Bath

YORK
Norwich
Oneonta
Catskill
Troy
Albany
Greenfield
Leominster
Fitchburg
Nashua
Lowell
Manchester
Haverhill
Lawrence
C. Ann
Newburyport

Johnson City
Binghamton
Catskill
Mts
Kingston
1281 ▲
Northampton
MASS.
Cambridge
BOSTON
Quincy
Cape Cod

Delaware
Poughkeepsie
Newburgh
Hudson
Pittsfield
Chicopee
Springfield
Worcester
Brockton

Carbondale
Dunmore
Middletown
Beacon
Danbury
Hartford
New Britain
Waterbury
Meriden
Woonsocket
Pawtucket
Providence
Warwick
Taunton
Fall River
New
Bedford
Martha's
Vineyard
Nantucket

Wilkes
Barre
Hazelton
Easton
Bethlehem
Paterson
Jersey City
Newark
Elizabeth
Yonkers
Mount
Vernon
New-
Bridgeport
Stamford
New-
Haven
New
London
CONN.   **R.I.**
Newport
Block I.

Reading
Norristown
Pottstown
NEW YORK
New Brunswick
Long Island
Long Branch
Asbury Park
Riverhead

Lancaster
Chester
Camden
NEW
JERSEY
Trenton

PHILA
Wilmington
Hammonton
Vineland
Bridgeton
Millville
Atlantic City
Ocean City

Cambridge
Milford
Henlopen
Cape May
DELAWARE
Seaford
Dover
Ocean City

Snow Hill
Salisbury

Acomac
Cape Charles
C. Charles

A   **T**   **L**   **A**   **N**   **T**   **I**   **C**
O   **C**   **E**   **A**   **N**

West from Greenwich
74   72   70   68   66   64

1   2   3   4   5   6   7

A

San Diego
Tijuana
Ensenada
Pt. Baja
3078
Pt. Sta.
Eugenia
C. San Lucas

Yuma
Phoenix
Mexicali
Tucson
Nogales
Agua Prieta
Ciudad Juárez   El Paso
Sonora
3200

Hermosillo
Empalme
Guaymas
Sta. Rosalia
Tiburón
Ciudad
Obregón
Navojoa
Los Mochis
Guamúchil

B

UNITED   STATE

Carlsbad   Wichita Falls
Fort Worth   Dallas
Abilene   Shreveport   Jackson   Birmingham
Carlsbad   Monroe   Montgomery
San Angelo   Tyler   Alabama
Waco   Alexandria   Baton Rouge   Mobile   Pensacola
Austin   Beaumont   Lake Charles   Lafayette   New Orleans   C. San
San Antonio   Houston   Port Arthur   Mississippi
Galveston   Blas
Delta

GULF OF MEXICO

C

3658
Pecos
Grande
Villa Ahumada
Chihuahua
Conchos
Delicias
Nueva Rosita
Piedras Negras   Eagle Pass
Hidalgo del   Sabinas
Parral   Monclova   Nuevo
Nazas   Falcon Res.   Laredo
3150   S. Pedro   Sabinas   Laredo
Gómez Palacio   Hidalgo   Reynosa   Matagorda I.
Torreón Saltillo   Monterrey   Corpus Christi
Concepcion   Montemorelos   Matamoros   Padre I.
del Oro   Brownsville
4054   Rio Grande del Norte
Victoria de   Matehuala   Victoria   Laguna de la Madre
Durango   Fresnillo   Ciudad
Mazatlán   Zacatecas   Mante   Tropic of Cancer
Rosario   San Luis   Ciudad   Yucatan
3353   Potosí   Madero   Pina
Aguascalientes   Tampico
Las Tres   3960   León   Panuco
Marías   Tepic   Irapuato   C. Rojo   Progreso   Valladolid   I. de
C. Corrientes   Guadalajara   Celaya   Querétaro   Tuxpan   Mérida   Cozumel
Ameca   L. de Chapala   Pachuca   Peto
Zamora   Gulf of   Campeche   Yucatan
Colima Vol.   MEXICO   Campeche   Chetumal
Manzanillo   Morelia   Toluca   Citlaltepetl 5700   Veracruz   Ciudad del Carmen   Laguna
Colima   Cuernavaca   Jalapa Enriquez   de Terminos
Balsas   Iguala Popocatepetl   Orizaba   Coatzacoalcos   Belize
3703   6452   Puebla   Minatitlán   Villahermosa   Belmopan   Turneffe Is.
Chilpancingo   Mexcala   3395   Isthmus of   BELIZE   Gulf of Hon
Acapulco   Oaxaca   Tehuantepec   Tuxtla   Pto. Barrios   Pto. Cortés   Tela   La Ceiba
Ometepec   Verde   Gutierrez   Usumacinta   Zacapa   S. Pedro Sula
3139   San Cristobal   HONDURAS
Salina Cruz   Juchitan   GUATEMALA   Comayagua
Tonala Chiapa   Tegucigalpa
G. of   Tapachula   4217   Choluteca
Tehuantepec   Quezaltenango   Guatemala   Sta. Ana   NICARA
San Salvador   León   G. of Fonseca
EL SALVADOR   S. Miguel   Managua
Nicoya Pen.   Puntare
S.

D

E

PACIFIC   OCEAN

PANAMA CANAL 1:1 000 000

14
Colón   Coco Solo
Fort   Puerto Pilón
Sherman   Cristobal
Margarita
Gatun   Zorra   I. El Limón
Gatun Locks
Gatun Dam   Juan Gallegos
Escobal   Frijoles
Colorado   Darien
The Gaillard Cut   Chagres   Gamboa
Balboa Hill   Madden Dam   Buenos Aires
350   Madden L.
Culebra
Paraiso
Pedro Miguel   Fort Clayton
Pedro Miguel Locks   Curundu
Miraflores Locks   Corozal
Arraijan   Balboa   Ancon
Fort Amador   Bay
La Chorrera   PANAMA   Panama
H   Madden L.   Chagres

0   10   20km

4   5   6

JAMAICA 1:5 000 000

Montego   Falmouth
Bay   St. Ann's Bay
Savanna   Galina Point
la Mar   Annotto Bay
Mandeville   Port Antonio
Kingston
2256   Morant
May Pen   Point
Spanish Town   Morant Bay
Portland
Point
J
K
15   16
17

78   77   76

TRINIDAD AND TOBAGO 1:5 000 000

Charlotteville
Tobago
Scarborough   R

Port of Spain
Arima
940   Sangre Grande
Rio   TRINIDAD
Gulf of Paria   Claro
San Fernando
Point Fortin   Princes Town
Siparia   S
Serpent's Mouth

19   20   21
61   60

0   50 km
Projection: Bonne

LEEWARD ISLANDS 1:5 000 000

The Valley   Anguilla (U.K.)   J
Marigot   St. Martin (Fr.)
St. Maarten   St. Barthélemy
(Neth.)   (Fr.)
Saba   St. Eustatius   Codrington   Barbuda
(Neth.)   (Neth.)   ANTIGUA
ST. KITTS &   &   K
NEVIS   BARBUDA
Basseterre   St. John's
Charlestown   Antigua
Redonda
Montserrat   L
Plymouth   (U.K.)   Guadeloupe Passage
GUADELOUPE   Grande Terre
(Fr.)   Ste Rose   Moule
Basse Terre   Désirade (Fr.)
Basse Terre   Pointe-à-Pitre
I. des Saintes   Marie-Galante
(Fr.)   Dominica   Grand Bourg
Passage
Portsmouth
Morne Diablotin   DOMINICA   M
1490   (Windward Is.)
Roseau

18   19   20   21
63   62   61

0   50 km

WINDWARD ISLANDS 1:5 000 000

M
Martinique Passage
Mt. Pelée   Ste. Marie
1397
St. Pierre   Le François
Fort de France   MARTINIQUE   N
Lamentin   (Fr.)
Ste. Anne
St. Lucia Channel
Castries
Soufrière   ST. LUCIA
Vieux Fort
St. Vincent Passage   P
Soufrière   Georgetown   BARBADOS
ST. VINCENT   Kingstown   Speightstown
1178   &   Bridgetown
THE GRENADINES   Bequia   Mustique
Canouan   Q
Union   Carriacou   Hillsborough
Ronde
St.   840   Grenville
George's   GRENADA   R

22
20   21
60

0   50 km

1 : 15 000 000

100   0   100   200   300   400 miles
100   0   100   200   300   400   500   600 km

8   **9**   **10**   **11**

8   9   10   11   12   13

A

B

C

D

E

F

G

ATLANTIC OCEAN

Bermuda (U.K.)
Hamilton

Columbus
C. Fear
Atlanta
Augusta
Macon
Charleston
Savannah
bany
lahassee
Jacksonville
Daytona Beach
Orlando
C. Canaveral
Tampa
tersburg
West Palm Beach
L. Okeechobee
Grand
Bahama
I.
Freeport
Gt. Abaco I.
Miami
Fort
Lauderdale
New Providence I.
Eleuthera I.
C. Sable
Nassau
Cat I.
S. Salvador
Key West
BAHAMAS
Andros I.
Tropic of Cancer
Florida Str.
Havana
Matanzas
Cárdenas
Sagua la Grande
Sta. Clara
Long I.
Mayaguana
Acklins
Turks &
Caicos Is.
(U.K.)
C U B A
Cienfuegos
Sancti Spíritus
B. Camagüey
Morón
Ciego de Ávila
Holguín
Gt. Inagua
I.
I. de Juventud
Manzanillo
2000
Bayamo
Santiago
de Cuba
Guantánamo
Cap Haitien
Santiago
San Francisco
de Macorís
PUERTO RICO (U.S.A.)
St. Thomas (U.S.A.)
Charlotte Amalie
Virgin Is. (U.K.)
Anguilla
St. Martin (Fr. & Neth.)
Grand Cayman
(U.K.)
Gonaives
DOMINICAN
REP.
La Romana
San Juan
ST. KITTS & NEVIS
G R E A T E R
Windward Passage
H A I T I
3175
2280
Santo Domingo
Ponce
1338
Caguas
Mayagüez
St. Croix
(U.S.A.)
ANTIGUA &
BARBUDA
St. John's
Montego Bay
Santiago
de Cuba
Les Cayes
Barahona
Bani
Mona Passage
Montserrat (U.K.)
Guadeloupe (Fr.)
Pointe à Pitre
JAMAICA
Kingston
Port au Prince
Hispaniola
A N T I L L E S
Leeward
Islands
LESSER
DOMINICA
Martinique (Fr.)
Fort de France
Caratasca Lagoon
C. Gracias á Dios
C A R I B B E A N   S E A
A N T I L L E S
Windward
ST. VINCENT
ST. LUCIA
BARBADOS
Bridgetown
THE GRENADINES
Islands
GRENADA
Providencia
(Col.)
San Andrés
(Col.)
Pta. Gallinas
Gulf of Venezuela
Aruba (Neth.)
Curaçao
Willemstad
Bonaire
Pen. de la
Guajira
Pen. de
Paraguaná
NETH.
ANTILLES
La Blanquilla
(Ven.)
Margarita
Tobago
Port of Spain
TRINIDAD & TOBAGO
Mosquito Coast
Bluefields
agua
Santa Marta
Barranquilla
5800
Sierra Nevada
de Santa Marta
Punta
Fijo
Coro
La Tortuga
(Ven.)
Carúpano
Cumaná
G. of
Paria
San Fernando
Cartagena
Sincelejo
G. of
Darién
L. de
Maracaibo
Maracaibo
Cabimas
Maracay
Valencia
Caracas
Barcelona
2596
Maturín
Delta of the
Orinoco
Limón
Colón
Vol. Barú
3374
Panama
Azuero
Pen.
Coiba
G. of
Panama
Atrato
Cauca
Valera
Mérida
5007
Cord. de Mérida
Barinas
Barquisimeto
Apure
El Tigre
Ciudad
Bolívar
Orinoco
Ciudad
Guayana
Georgetown
New
Amsterdam
RICA
David
Quibdó
Medellín
Barrancabermeja
3960
Cúcuta
4100
San Cristóbal
Bucaramanga
Arauca
Arauca
San Fernando
de Apure
Pto. Ayacucho
V E N E Z U E L A
Angel
Falls
2560
Roraima
2810
Cuyuni
Paragua
G U Y A N A
Essequibo
Corentyne
SURINAM
1280
Manizales
Pereira
Tunja
Meta
2285
Caura
Sierra Pacaraima
Buenaventura
Armenia
Olima 5215
Girardot
Bogotá
C O L O M B I A
Guaviare
Sa. Parima
Casiquiare
Cali 5750
Guaviare
Popayán
4646
Magdalena
B R A Z I L

West from Greenwich   80   75   70   65   60

COPYRIGHT. GEORGE PHILIP & SON. LTD.

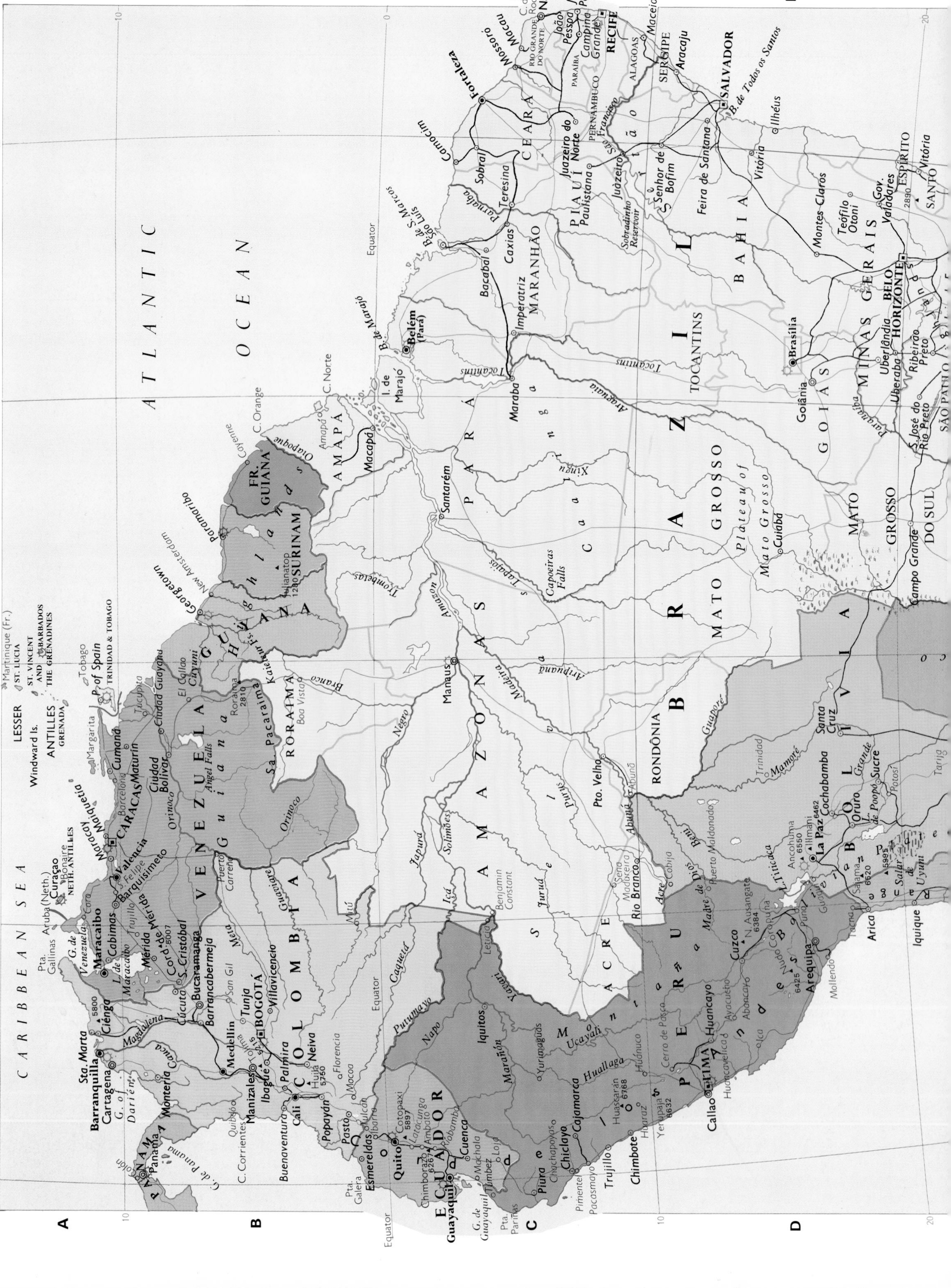

A B C D

6

5

4

3

2

1

ATLANTIC OCEAN

CARIBBEAN SEA

LESSER ANTILLES
Windward Is.
GRENADA
Martinique (Fr.)
ST. LUCIA
ST. VINCENT
BARBADOS
AND THE GRENADINES
Tobago
P. of Spain
TRINIDAD & TOBAGO
Margarita I.
Curaçao (Neth.)
Aruba (Neth.)
NETH. ANTILLES
Bonaire

VENEZUELA
Maracaibo
Caracas
Valencia
Barquisimeto
Maturín
Cumaná
Barcelona
Ciudad Bolívar
Ciudad Guayana
El Callao
Angel Falls
Orinoco

COLOMBIA
BOGOTÁ
Medellín
Cali
Manizales
Barranquilla
Cartagena
Sta. Marta
Cúcuta
Bucaramanga
Ibagué
Palmira
Neiva
Pasto
Popayán
Quibdó
Buenaventura
Villavicencio
Florencia

PANAMA
Panama
Colón

ECUADOR
Quito
Guayaquil
Cuenca
Machala
Ambato
Esmeraldas
Cotopaxi
Chimborazo

GUYANA
Georgetown
New Amsterdam

SURINAM
Paramaribo

FR. GUIANA
Cayenne

Guiana Highlands
RORAIMA

PERU
LIMA
Callao
Arequipa
Trujillo
Chiclayo
Chimbote
Iquitos
Cuzco
Piura
Huancayo
Cajamarca
Ayacucho
Ica
Cerro de Pasco
Huánuco
Huaraz
Mollendo

BRAZIL
Brasília
Recife
Salvador
Fortaleza
Belém (Pará)
Belo Horizonte
Natal
João Pessoa
Maceió
Aracaju
Teresina
São Luís
Manaus
Santarém
Macapá
Imperatriz
Marabá
Sobral
Caxias
Cuiabá
Pôrto Velho
Rio Branco
Goiânia
Uberlândia
Uberaba
Ribeirão Preto
Vitória
Gov. Valadares
Montes Claros
Teófilo Otoni
Feira de Santana
Ilhéus
Campina Grande
Juazeiro do Norte
Mossoró
Camocim

MARANHÃO
PIAUÍ
CEARÁ
PERNAMBUCO
PARAÍBA
ALAGOAS
SERGIPE
BAHIA
MINAS GERAIS
ESPÍRITO SANTO
GOIÁS
TOCANTINS
PARÁ
AMAPÁ
AMAZONAS
RONDÔNIA
ACRE
MATO GROSSO
MATO GROSSO DO SUL
Plateau of Mato Grosso

BOLIVIA
La Paz
Sucre
Santa Cruz
Cochabamba
Oruro
Potosí
L. Titicaca
L. de Poopó
Salar de Uyuni

Amazon
Negro
Madeira
Tapajós
Xingu
Tocantins
Purus
Juruá
Putumayo
Napo
Marañón
Ucayali
Huallaga
Magdalena
Orinoco

Equator

I : 20 000 000

100   0   100   200   300   400 miles
100   0   100   200   300   400   500   600   km

RIO DE JANEIRO
C. Frio
Niterói
Sto André
SÃO PAULO
Santos
Curitiba
Ponta Grossa
Londrina
PARANÁ
Iguaçu Falls
Itaipú Dam
Concepción
Asunción
PARAGUAY
Paraguay
Pilcomayo
Formosa
Pilar
Resistencia
Corrientes
Paraná
Posadas
Uruguay
SANTA CATARINA
Florianópolis
C. Sta. Marta Grande
Lajes
RIO GRANDE DO SUL
Caxias do Sul
Pôrto Alegre
Sta. Maria
Pelotas
Lagoa dos Patos
L. Mirim
Melo
Tacuarembó
URUGUAY
Artigas
Rivera
Salto
Paysandú
Fray Bentos
Mercedes
S. José
Durazno
Florida
Treinta y Tres
Rocha
Maldonado
MONTEVIDEO
Río de la Plata
Mar del Plata
C. Corrientes

PACIFIC

OCEAN

I. San Félix (Chile)
I. San Ambrosio
Antofagasta
Copiapó
Coquimbo
Is. Juan Fernández (Chile)
Tropic of Capricorn

ATLANTIC

OCEAN

South Georgia (U.K.)

Viña del Mar
Valparaíso
SANTIAGO
Rancagua
Talca
Chillán
Concepción
Talcahuano
Los Angeles
Temuco
Valdivia
Osorno
Pto. Montt
Chiloé
C. Quilán
Chonos Arch.
G. de Peñas
I. Wellington
Queen Adelaide Arch.
Magellan's Str.
I. Santa Inés
Pta. Arenas
Tierra del Fuego
C. Horn
Beagle Chan.
Ushuaia
C. Vírgenes
Magellan's Str.
Río Gallegos
B. Grande
S. Lorenzo
S. Valentín 4058
Pto. Deseado
C. Tres Puntas
Deseado
Golfo San Jorge
Comodoro Rivadavia
Chubut
Trelew
Valdés Pen.
Golfo San Matías
B. Blanca
Trinidad
Bahía Blanca
Colorado
Río Negro
C. de Bariloche
Neuquén
San Rafael
San Luis
Mendoza
Aconcagua 7020
Jáchal
S. Juan
La Rioja
Catamarca
Cerro del Toro 6380
Ojos del Salado 6863
Copiapó 6250
Famatina 6250
Calama
San Salvador de Jujuy
Salta
San Miguel de Tucumán
Santiago del Estero
Salinas Grandes
Salado
Córdoba
Sa. de Córdoba
Río Cuarto
Santa Fe
Rosario
Paraná
BUENOS AIRES
La Plata
Avellaneda
Santa Rosa
Salado
Colorado
Desierto
Atacama
5970
6723
Llullaillaco
PUNA

ATLANTIC

Falkland Is. (U.K.)
W. Falkland
Stanley
E. Falkland

Projection : Lambert's Equivalent Azimuthal
West from Greenwich

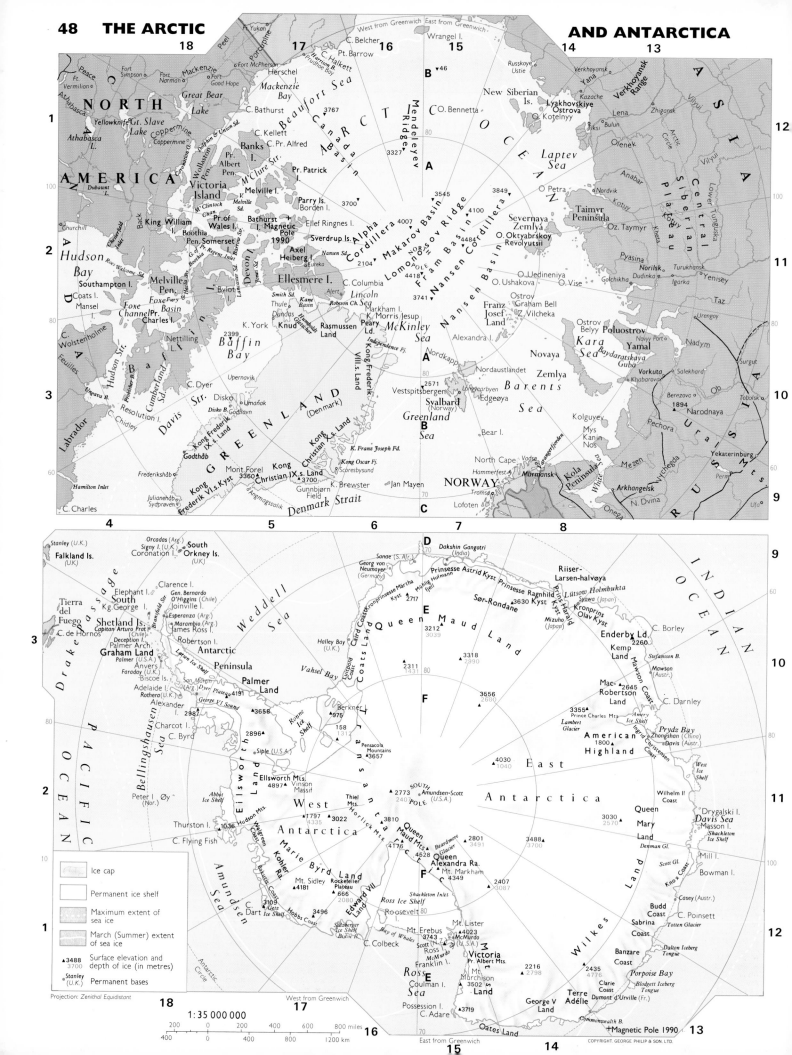

18   17   16   15   14   13

West from Greenwich   East from Greenwich

NORTH AMERICA

Peace, Ft. Vermilion, Athabasca L., Peel, Ft. Yukon, Pt. Yukon, Porcupine, Fort McPherson, C. Belcher, Wrangel I., Russkoye Ustie, Verkhoyansk, Yana, Verkhoyansk Range, Vilyui

Ft. Simpson, Fort Norman, Ft. Good Hope, Mackenzie, Great Bear Lake, Herschel I., Mackenzie Bay, C. Halkett, Harrison B., Pt. Barrow, Prudhoe Bay, C. Bennetta, New Siberian Is., Lyakhovskiye Ostrova, O. Kotelnyy, Zhigansk

Yellowknife, Gt. Slave Lake, Coppermine, Coppermine, C. Bathurst, Beaufort Sea, 3767, Mendeleyev Ridge, 46, O. Bennetta, Lena, Bulun, Olenek, **ASIA**

1   Athabasca L., Dubawnt L., Gt. Slave Lake, C. Kellett, C. Pr. Alfred, Banks I., Canada Basin, 3327, Laptev Sea, Tiksi, Anabar, Kotuy, Lower Tunguska **12**

AMERICA   Churchill, Victoria Island, M'Clintock Chan., Melville I., Melville Sd., Pr. Patrick, Pr. Patrick I., 3700, Borden I., 3545, 3849, Alpha Cordillera, 4007, Makarov Basin, 4100, Severnaya Zemlya, O. Oktyabrskoy Revolyutsii, O. Petra, Nordvik, Taimyr Peninsula, Oz. Taymyr, Khatanga, Central Siberian Plateau

King William I., Boothia Pen., Pr. of Wales I., Bathurst I., Magnetic Pole 1990, Ellef Ringnes I., Sverdrup Is., Lomonosov Ridge, Fram Basin, 4484, Nansen Cordillera, Novaya Zemlya, Norilsk, Dudinka, Turukhansk

2   Hudson Bay, Somerset I., Axel Heiberg I., Nansen Sd., 2104, NORTH POLE, 4418, Nansen Basin, Franz Josef Land, O. Ushakova, O. Vise, O. Uedineniya, Yenisey, Igarka, Taz **11**

Southampton I., Coats I., Mansel I., Melville Pen., Foxe Basin, Devon I., Ellesmere I., C. Columbia, Alert, 3741, Ostrov Graham Bell, Z. Vilcheka, Kara Sea, Golchikha

Chesterfield Inlet, Foxe Channel, Pr. Charles I., Bylot I., Lancaster Sd., Smith Sd., Thule, Kane Basin, Robeson Ch., Lincoln Sea, Markham I., K. Morris Jesup, Peary Ld., McKinley Sea, Alexandra I., Nordaustlandet, Zemlya, Ostrov Belyy, Poluostrov Yamal, Urengoy

BAFFIN Feuilles, Ungava B., Hudson Str., Resolution I., C. Chidley, Labrador, Cumberland Sd., Baffin Bay, 2399, K. York, Knud Rasmussen Land, Kong Frederik VIII.s Land, Independence Fj., Nordkapp, Svalbard (Norway), Vestspitsbergen, Longyearbyen, Edgeøya, Barents Sea, Novaya Zemlya, Baydaratskaya Guba, Nadym, Vorkuta, Khabarovo, Surgut

3   C. Dyer, Disko, Upernavik, Umanak, Disko B., Godhavn, 2571, Bear I., Greenland Sea, North Cape, Kolguyev, Mys Kanin Nos, Pechora, Berezova, 1894, Narodnaya, Tobolsk **10**

Davis Str., Godthåb, Kong Frederik IX.s Land, GREENLAND (Denmark), Mont Forel, 3360, Kong Christian IX.s Land, Kong Christian X.s Land, K. Franz Joseph Fd., Kong Oscar Fj., Scoresbysund, Jan Mayen, Hammerfest, Vadsø, Varangerfjorden, Murmansk, Kola Peninsula, White Sea, Mezen, Arkhangelsk, Vychegda, Yekaterinburg, Ural Mts., Perm

RUSSIA

C. Charles, Frederikshåb, Kong Frederik VI.s Kyst, Julianehåb, Sydprøven, Angmagssalik, Gunnbjørn Field, K. Brewster, Denmark Strait, Hamilton Inlet, Denmark Strait, **NORWAY**, Tromsø, Lofoten, Bodø, Onega, N. Dvina, Ufa

4   5   6   7   8

---

9   Stanley (U.K.), Falkland Is. (U.K.), Orcadas (Arg.), Signy I. (U.K.), Coronation I., South Orkney Is. (U.K.), Dakshin Gangotri (India), Sanae (S. Afr.), Georg von Neumayer (Germany), Prinsesse Astrid Kyst, Prinsesse Ragnhild Kyst, Riiser-Larsen-halvøya, **INDIAN OCEAN**

Tierra del Fuego, C. de Hornos, Elephant I., Clarence I., South Shetland Is., Kg. George I., O'Higgins (Chile), Gen. Bernardo, Joinville I., Esperanza (Arg.), Marambio (Arg.), James Ross I., Capitan Arturo Prat (Chile), Deception I., Palmer Arch., Weddell Sea, Kronprinsesse Martha Kyst, 2717, Mühlig Hofmann fjell, Sør-Rondane, 3630, Lützow Holmbukta, Prins Harald Kyst, Syowa (Japan), Kronprins Olav Kyst, C. Borley

3   Graham Land, Palmer (U.S.A.), Anvers I., Faraday (U.K.), Biscoe Is., Robertson I., Antarctic Peninsula, Larsen Ice Shelf, Coats Land, Caird Coast, Queen Maud Land, Mizuho (Japan), 3212, 3039, Enderby Ld., 2260, Kemp Land, Stefansson B. **10**

Adelaide I., Rothera (U.K.), San Martin (Arg.), Palmer Land, Dyer Plateau, 4191, Vahsel Bay, 3318, 2990, Mawson Coast, Mawson (Austr.), C. Darnley

Alexander I., 2987, George VI Sound, 3658, Ronne Ice Shelf, Berkner I., 975, 3556, 2600, Mac-Robertson Land, 2645, Prince Charles Mts., 3355, Amery Ice Shelf

2   Charcot I., C. Byrd, 2896, Ellsworth Land, 158, 1312, Pensacola Mountains, 3657, Lambert Glacier, 1040, 4030, East, 1800, Zhongshan (China), Davis (Austr.), Prydz Bay, Ingrid Christensen Coast **11**

Bellingshausen Sea, Siple (U.S.A.), American Highland, West Ice Shelf

Peter I. Øy (Nor.), Ellsworth Mts., 4897, Vinson Massif, 2773, SOUTH POLE, Amundsen-Scott (U.S.A.), 240, Antarctica, Wilhelm II Coast

PACIFIC OCEAN   Thurston I., 1036, Hudson Mts., 1797, 4335, 3022, Thiel Mts., Horlick Mts., 3810, Queen Maud Mts., 3030, 2570, Queen Mary Land, Drygalski I., Davis Sea, Masson I.

C. Flying Fish, Marie Byrd Land, Kohler Ra., West Antarctica, 4176, 4528, Queen Alexandra Ra., Beardmore Glacier, 2801, 3491, 3488, 3700, Denman Gl., Shackleton Ice Shelf

1   Amundsen Sea, Mt. Sidley, 4181, Rockefeller Plateau, 666, Edward VII Land, 2080, Mt. Markham, 4349, 2407, 3087, Scott Gl., Knox Coast, Bowman I., Mill I. **12**

C. Dart, 3109, Getz Ice Shelf, 3496, Hobbs Coast, Shackleton Inlet, Roosevelt I., Ross Ice Shelf, Mt. Erebus, 4023, McMurdo (U.S.A.), Budd Coast, C. Poinsett, Sabrina Coast, Totten Glacier

Bakutis Coast, Sulzberger Ice Shelf, Bay of Whales, Mt. Lister, 3743, Ross I., Scott (N.Z.), Victoria Land, Wilkes Land, Dalton Iceberg Tongue, Banzare Coast

Antarctic Circle, C. Colbeck, McMurdo Sd., Franklin I., Pr. Albert Mts., 2216, 2798, 2435, 4776, Clarie Coast, Blodgett Iceberg Tongue

Ross Sea, Coulman I., 3502, 3719, Mt. Murchison, Terre Adélie (Fr.), Dumont d'Urville (Fr.), Porpoise Bay

Possession I., C. Adare, George V Land, Oates Land, Commonwealth B., Magnetic Pole 1990

Legend

- Ice cap
- Permanent ice shelf
- Maximum extent of sea ice
- March (Summer) extent of sea ice
- ▲3488 / 3700   Surface elevation and depth of ice (in metres)
- ▪ Stanley (U.K.)   Permanent bases

Projection: Zenithal Equidistant

1:35 000 000

200   0   200   400   600   800 miles
400   0   400   800   1200 km

COPYRIGHT. GEORGE PHILIP & SON. LTD.

INDEX

The index contains the names of all the principal places and features shown on the maps. The alphabetical order of names composed of two or more words is governed primarily by the first word and then by the second. This is an example of the rule:

New South Wales □ **34** G8
New York □ **43** D9
New York City **43** E11
New Zealand ■ **35** J13
Newark, Del., U.S.A. **43** F10

Physical features composed of a proper name (Erie) and a description (Lake) are positioned alphabetically by the proper name. The description is positioned after the proper name and is usually abbreviated:

Erie, L. **42** D7

Where a description forms part of a settlement or administrative name, however, it is always written in full and put in its true alphabetical position:

Mount Isa **34** E6

Names beginning with M' and Mc are indexed as if they were spelt Mac. Names beginning St. are alphabetized under Saint, but Santa and San are all spelt in full and are alphabetized accordingly. If the same placename occurs two or more times in the index and all are in the same country, each is followed by the name of the administrative subdivision in which it is located. The names are placed in the alphabetical order of the subdivision. For example:

Columbus, Ga., U.S.A. **41** D10
Columbus, Ind., U.S.A. **42** F5
Columbus, Ohio, U.S.A. **42** F6

The number in bold type which follows each name in the index refers to the number of the map page where that feature or place will be found. This is usually the largest scale at which the place or feature appears.

The letter and figure which are in lighter type immediately after the page number give the grid square on the map page, within which the feature is situated. The letter represents the latitude and the figure the longitude. In some cases the feature itself may fall within the specified square, while the name is outside.

Rivers are indexed to their mouths or confluences, and carry the symbol → after their names. A solid square ■ follows the name of a country, while an open square □ refers to a first order administrative area.

Aachen **10** C4
Aalborg **6** G9
Aarau **10** E5
Aare → **10** E5
Aarhus **6** G10
Abadan **24** B3
Abbeville **8** A4
Abéché **29** F9
Abeokuta **30** C2
Aberdeen **7** C5
Abidjan **28** G4
Abitibi L. **42** A8
Abkhazia □ **15** F7
Abohar **23** D5
Abu Dhabi **24** C4
Abuja **30** C3
Acapulco **44** D5
Accomac **43** G10
Accra **30** C1
Acklins I. **45** C10
Aconcagua **47** F3
Acre □ **46** C2
Adamawa Highlands **29** G7
Adana **15** G6
Adapazarı **15** F5
Addis Ababa **29** G12
Adelaide, Australia **34** G6
Adelaide, S. Africa **31** C4
Aden **24** D3
Aden, G. of **24** D3
Adirondack Mts. **43** D10
Admiralty Is. **36** H6
Ado-Ekiti **30** C3
Adoni **25** D6
Adour → **8** E3
Adrar **28** C4
Adrian **42** E5
Adriatic Sea **12** C6
Ægean Sea **13** E11
Afghanistan ■ **24** B5
'Afif **24** C3
Agadès **30** A3
Agadir **28** B3
Agartala **23** H13
Agen **8** D4
Agra **23** F6
Agrigento **12** F5
Aguascalientes **44** C4
Agulhas, C. **31** C3
Ahmadabad **23** H4
Ahmadnagar **25** D6
Ahmadpur **23** E3
Ahvaz **24** B3
Ahvenanmaa Is. **6** F11
Aïr **28** E6
Aisne → **8** B5
Aix-en-Provence **8** E6
Aix-les-Bains **8** D6
Ajaccio **8** F8
Ajanta Ra. **23** J5
Ajaria □ **15** F7
Ajmer **23** F5
Akashi **19** B4
Akita **19** A7
Akola **23** J6
Akranes **6** B2
Akron **42** E7
Aktyubinsk **15** D10
Akure **30** C3
Akureyri **6** B4
Al Ḥudaydah **24** D3
Al Hufūf **24** C3
Al Jawf **24** C2
Al Kut **24** B3
Al Qatif **24** C3
Al 'Ula **24** C2
Alabama □ **41** D9
Aland Is. = Ahvenanmaa Is. **6** F11
Alaska □ **38** B5
Alaska, G. of **38** C5
Alaska Peninsula **38** C4
Alaska Range **38** B4
Alba-Iulia **11** E12
Albacete **9** C5
Albania ■ **13** D9
Albany, Australia **34** H2
Albany, Ga., U.S.A. **41** D10
Albany, N.Y., U.S.A. **43** D11
Albany → **39** C11
Albert L. **32** D6
Alberta □ **38** C8
Albertville **8** D7
Albi **8** E5
Albion **42** D5
Albuquerque **40** C5
Albury **34** H8
Alcalá de Henares **9** B4
Aldabra Is. **27** G8
Aldan → **18** C14
Aleksandrovsk-Sakhalinskiy **18** D16
Alençon **8** B4
Alès **8** D6
Alessándria **12** B3
Ålesund **6** F9
Aleutian Is. **36** B10
Alexander Arch. **38** C6
Alexandria, Egypt **29** B10
Alexandria, La., U.S.A. **41** D8
Alexandria, Va., U.S.A. **42** F9
Algarve **9** D1
Algeciras **9** D3
Algeria ■ **28** C5
Algiers **28** A5
Alicante **9** C5
Alice Springs **34** E5
Aligarh **23** F7
Alipur Duar **23** F12
Aliquippa **42** E7
Aliwal North **31** C4
Alkmaar **10** B3
Allahabad **23** G8
Allegan **42** D5
Allegheny → **42** E8
Allegheny Plateau **42** G7
Allentown **43** E10
Alleppey **25** E6
Allier → **8** C5
Alma **42** D5
Almaty **18** E9
Almelo **10** B4
Almería **9** D4
Alor **22** D4
Alpena **42** C6
Alps **10** E5
Alsace **8** B7
Altai **20** B4
Altay **20** B3
Altoona **42** E8
Altun Shan **20** C3
Alwar **23** F6
Amadjuak L. **39** B12
Amagasaki **19** B4
Amarillo **40** C6
Amazon → **46** C4
Ambala **23** D6
Ambikapur **23** H9
Ambon **22** D4
American Samoa ■ **35** C17
Amiens **8** B5
Amman **24** B2
Amos **42** A8
Amravati **23** J6
Amreli **23** J3
Amritsar **23** D5
Amroha **23** E7
Amsterdam, Neths. **10** B3
Amsterdam, U.S.A. **43** D10
Amudarya → **18** E7
Amundsen Gulf **38** A7
Amundsen Sea **48** E1
Amur → **18** D16
An Najaf **24** B3
An Nasiriyah **24** B3
An Nhon **22** B2
Anadyr **18** C19
Anadyr, G. of **18** C20
Anaheim **40** D3
Anambas Is. **22** C2
Anantnag **23** C5
Anar **24** B4
Anatolia **15** G5
Anchorage **38** B5
Ancona **12** C5
Anda **21** B7
Andalucía □ **9** D3
Andaman Is. **25** D8
Anderson **42** E5
Andes **46** E3
Andhra Pradesh □ **25** D6
Andorra ■ **9** A6
Andreanof Is. **38** C2
Ándria **12** D7
Andros I. **45** C9
Angara → **18** D11
Ange **6** F11
Angel Falls **46** B3
Angerman → **6** F11
Angers **8** C3
Anglesey **7** E4
Angola ■ **33** G3
Angoulême **8** D4
Angoumois **8** D3
Anguilla ■ **44** J18
Anhui □ **21** C6
Anjou **8** C3
Ankara **15** G5
Ann, C. **43** D12
Ann Arbor **42** D6
Annaba **28** A6
Annapolis **42** F9
Annecy **8** D7
Annobón **27** G4
Anshun **20** D5
Antalya **15** G5
Antananarivo **33** H9
Antarctic Pen. **48** D4
Antibes **8** E7
Anticosti I. **43** A16
Antigua Barbuda ■ **44** K20
Antofagasta **47** E2
Antsiranana **33** G9
Antwerp **10** C3
Anyang **21** C6
Aomori **19** F12
Aparri **22** B4
Apeldoorn **10** B3
Apennines **12** B4
Apia **35** C16
Appalachian Mts. **42** G7
Appleton **42** C3
Aqmola **18** D9
Ar Ramadi **24** B3
Arabian Desert **29** C11
Arabian Gulf = Gulf, The **24** C4
Arabian Sea **24** D5
Aracaju **46** D6
Arad **11** E11
Arafura Sea **22** D5
Aragón □ **9** B5
Araguaia → **46** C5
Arak **24** B3
Arakan Yoma **25** C8
Aral **18** E8
Aral Sea **18** E8
Arcachon **8** D3
Arctic Ocean **48** B17
Arctic Red River **38** B6
Ardabil **24** B3
Ardennes **10** D3
Arendal **6** G9
Arequipa **46** D2
Argentan **8** B3
Argentina ■ **47** F3
Arima **44** S20
Arizona □ **40** D4
Arkansas □ **41** D8
Arkansas → **41** D8
Arkhangelsk **14** B7
Arles **8** E6
Arlington **42** F9
Arlon **10** D3
Armenia ■ **15** F7
Arnhem **10** C3
Arnhem Land **34** C5
Arnprior **42** C9
Arrah **23** G10
Arran **7** D4
Arras **8** A5
Artois **8** A5
Aru Is. **22** D5
Arunachal Pradesh □ **25** C8
Arusha **32** E7
Asab **31** B2
Asahigawa **19** F12
Asansol **23** H11
Asbestos **43** C12
Asbury Park **43** E10
Ascension I. **27** G2
Ashkhabad **18** F7
Ashland, Ky., U.S.A. **42** F6
Ashland, Ohio, U.S.A. **42** E6
Ashtabula **42** E7
Asifabad **23** K7
Asir □ **24** D3
Asmara **29** E12
Assam □ **23** F13
Assen **10** B4
Assisi **12** C5
Asti **12** B3
Astrakhan **15** E8
Asturias □ **9** A3
Asunción **47** E4
Aswân **29** D11
Atacama Desert **47** E3
Atbara **29** E11
Atbara → **29** E11
Athabasca → **38** C8
Athabasca, L. **38** C9
Athens, Greece **13** F10
Athens, U.S.A. **42** F6
Atikokan **42** A2
Atlanta **41** D10
Atlantic City **43** F10
Atlantic Ocean **2** E9
Atyraū **18** E7
Au Sable → **42** C6
Aube → **8** B5
Auburn, Ind., U.S.A. **42** E5
Auburn, N.Y., U.S.A. **42** D9
Aubusson **8** D5
Auch **8** E4
Auckland **35** H13
Aude → **8** E5
Augrabies Falls **31** B3
Augsburg **10** D6
Augusta, Ga., U.S.A. **41** D10
Augusta, Maine, U.S.A. **43** C13
Aunis **8** C3
Aurangabad, Bihar, India **23** G10
Aurangabad, Maharashtra, India **23** K5
Aurillac **8** D5
Aurora **42** E3
Austin **40** D7
Australia ■ **34** E5
Australian Alps **34** H8
Australian Capital Territory □ **34** H8
Austria ■ **10** E8
Autun **8** C6
Auvergne **8** D5
Auxerre **8** C5
Avallon **8** C5
Avellino **12** D6
Avignon **8** E6
Ávila **9** B3
Avranches **8** B3
Axiós → **13** D10
Ayers Rock **34** F5
Ayr **7** D4
Azamgarh **23** F9
Azerbaijan ■ **15** F8
Azores **2** C8
Azov, Sea of **15** E6
Azuero Pen. **45** F8
Babol **24** B4
Babuyan Chan. **22** B4
Bacău **11** E14
Bacolod **22** B4
Bad Axe **42** D6
Badajoz **9** C2
Badalona **9** B7
Baden-Württemberg □ **10** D5
Baffin I. **39** B12
Baghdad **24** B3
Baguio **22** B4
Bahamas ■ **45** C10
Baharampur **23** G12
Bahawalpur **23** E3
Bahía = Salvador **46** D6
Bahía □ **46** D5
Bahía Blanca **47** F3
Bahraich **23** F8
Bahrain ■ **24** C4
Baia Mare **11** E12
Baie-St-Paul **43** B12
Baikal, L. **18** D12
Baja California **44** B2
Bakersfield **40** C3
Bakhtaran **24** B3
Baku **15** F8
Balabac Str. **22** C3
Balaghat **23** J8
Balaton **11** E9
Balboa **44** H14
Baldwin **42** D5
Balearic Is. **9** C7
Baleshwar **23** J11
Bali **22** D3
Balikeşir **13** E12
Balikpapan **22** D3
Balkan Mts. **13** C10
Balkhash, L. **18** E9
Ballarat **34** H7
Balqash **18** E9
Balrampur **23** F9
Balsas → **44** D4
Baltic Sea **6** G11
Baltimore **42** F9
Bam **24** C4
Bamako **28** F3
Bamberg **10** D6
Bamenda **30** C4
Bancroft **42** C9
Banda **23** G8
Banda Aceh **22** C1
Banda Is. **22** D4
Banda Sea **22** D4
Bandar Abbas **24** C4
Bandar Khomeyni **24** B3
Bandar Seri Begawan **22** C3
Bandundu **32** E3
Bandung **22** D2
Bangalore **25** D6
Banggai Arch. **22** D4
Bangka **22** D2
Bangka Str. **22** D2
Bangkok **22** B2
Bangladesh ■ **23** H13
Bangor **43** C13
Bangui **32** D3
Bangweulu, L. **32** G6
Banja Luka **12** B7
Banjarmasin **22** D3
Banjul **28** F1
Banks I. **38** A7
Bankura **23** H11
Bannu **23** C3
Banská Bystrica **11** D10
Banyak Is. **22** C1
Baoding **21** C6
Baoji **20** C5
Baotou **21** B6
Bar Harbor **43** C13
Bar-le-Duc **8** B6
Baracaldo **9** A4
Baramula **23** B5
Baran **23** G6
Baranovichi **11** B14
Barbados ■ **44** P22
Barberton, S. Africa **31** B5
Barberton, U.S.A. **42** E7
Barcelona **9** B7
Barddhaman **23** H11
Bardstown **42** G5
Bareilly **23** E7
Barents Sea **48** B8
Barhi **23** G10
Bari **12** D7
Bari Doab **23** D4
Barisal **23** H13
Barito → **22** D3
Barkly Tableland **34** D6
Barkly West **31** B3
Barletta **12** D7
Barmer **23** G3
Barnaul **18** D10
Barques, Pt. Aux **42** C6
Barquísimeto **46** A3
Barrancabermeja **46** B2
Barranquilla **46** A2
Barre **43** C11
Barrie **42** C8
Barry's Bay **42** C9
Bashkortostan □ **14** D10
Basilan **22** C4
Baskatong, Rés. **43** B10
Basle **10** E4
Basque Provinces = País Vasco □ **9** A4
Basra **24** B3
Bass Str. **34** H8
Basse-Terre **44** M20
Bassein **25** D8
Basseterre **44** K19
Basti **23** F9
Bastia **8** E8
Bata **32** D1
Batangas **22** B4
Batavia **42** D8
Bath, U.K. **7** F5
Bath, Maine, U.S.A. **43** D13
Bath, N.Y., U.S.A. **42** D9
Bathurst, Australia **34** G8
Bathurst, Canada **43** B15
Batna **28** A6
Baton Rouge **41** D8
Battambang **22** B2
Batticaloa **25** E7
Battle Creek **42** D5
Batu Is. **22** D1
Batu Pahat **22** C2
Batumi **15** F7
Bavaria = Bayern □ **10** D6
Bawean **22** D3
Bay City **42** D6
Bayamo **45** C9
Bayan Har Shan **20** C4
Bayern □ **10** D6
Bayeux **8** B3
Bayonne **8** E3
Bayrūt **24** B2
Beacon **43** E11
Beagle, Canal **47** H3
Béarn **8** E3
Beauce, Plaine de la **8** B4
Beaufort Sea **48** B18
Beaufort West **31** C3
Beauharnois **43** C11
Beaumont **41** D8
Beaune **8** C6
Beauvais **8** B5
Beaver Falls **42** E7
Beaver I. **42** C5
Beawar **23** F5
Béchar **28** B4
Beckley **42** G7
Bedford, Ind., U.S.A. **42** F4
Bedford, Va., U.S.A. **42** G8
Bei'an **21** B7
Beijing **21** C6
Beira **33** H6
Békéscsaba **11** E11
Bela **23** F1
Belarus ■ **11** B14
Belau = Palau ■ **36** G5
Belaya Tserkov **11** D16
Belcher Is. **39** C12
Belém **46** C5
Belfast, S. Africa **31** B5
Belfast, U.K. **7** D4
Belfast, U.S.A. **43** C13
Belfort **8** C7
Belgaum **25** D6
Belgium ■ **10** C3
Belgorod **15** D6
Belgrade **13** B9
Beliton Is. **22** D2
Belize ■ **44** D7
Belize City **44** D7
Bellaire **42** E7
Bellary **25** D6
Belle-Ile **8** C2
Belle Isle, Str. of **39** C14
Bellefontaine **42** E6
Belleville **42** C9
Bellingshausen Sea **48** D3
Bellinzona **10** E5
Belmopan **44** D7
Belo Horizonte **46** D5

Belonia 23 H13
Belorussia = Belarus ■ 11 B14
Beltsy 11 E14
Belukha 18 E10
Ben Nevis 7 C4
Benares = Varanasi 23 G9
Bendigo 34 H7
Benevento 12 D6
Bengal, Bay of 23 K12
Bengbu 21 C6
Benghazi 29 B9
Bengkulu 22 D2
Beni Suef 29 C11
Benidorm 9 C5
Benin ■ 30 C2
Benin, Bight of 30 C2
Benin City 30 C3
Benoni 31 B4
Benton Harbor 42 D4
Benue → 30 C3
Benxi 21 B7
Berbérati 32 D3
Berea 42 G5
Bérgamo 12 B3
Bergen 6 F9
Bergerac 8 D4
Berhala Str. 22 D2
Berhampur 23 K10
Bering Sea 36 B9
Bering Strait 38 B3
Berlin, Germany 10 B7
Berlin, U.S.A. 43 C12
Bermuda ■ 45 A12
Berne 10 E4
Berry 8 C5
Berwick 42 E9
Berwick-upon-Tweed 7 D5
Besançon 8 C7
Bethal 31 B4
Bethlehem, S. Africa 31 B4
Bethlehem, U.S.A. 43 E10
Béthune 8 A5
Bettiah 23 F10
Betul 23 J6
Béziers 8 E5
Bhagalpur 23 G11
Bhandara 23 J7
Bhanrer Ra. 23 H7
Bharatpur 23 F6
Bhatinda 23 D5
Bhatpara 23 H12
Bhavnagar 23 J4
Bhilwara 23 G5
Bhima → 25 D6
Bhiwani 23 E6
Bhopal 23 H6
Bhubaneshwar 23 J10
Bhuj 23 H2
Bhusaval 23 J5
Bhutan ■ 23 F13
Biafra, B. of 26 F4
Biała Podlaska 11 B12
Białystok 11 B12
Biarritz 8 E3
Biddeford 43 D12
Bié Plateau 33 G3
Biel 10 E4
Bielefeld 10 B5
Bielsko-Biała 11 D10
Bien Hoa 22 B2
Big Rapids 42 D5
Bighorn Mts. 40 B5
Bihar 23 G10
Bihar □ 23 G10
Bikaner 23 E4
Bikini Atoll 36 F8
Bilaspur 23 H9
Bilbao 9 A4
Billings 40 A5
Bina-Etawah 23 G7
Binghamton 43 D10
Binjai 22 C1
Bioko 30 D3
Birmingham, U.K. 7 E6
Birmingham, U.S.A. 41 D9
Biscay, B. of 8 D1
Bishkek 18 E9
Bisho 31 C4
Biskra 28 B6
Bismarck Arch. 34 A9
Bissau 28 F1
Bitolj 13 D9
Bitterfontein 31 C2
Biwa-Ko 19 B5
Biysk 18 D10
Black Forest = Schwarzwald 10 D5
Black Sea 15 F6
Black Volta → 30 C1
Blackburn 7 E5
Blackpool 7 E5
Blacksburg 42 G7
Blagoveshchensk 18 D14
Blanc, Mont 8 D7
Blantyre 33 H6
Blenheim 35 J13
Blitar 22 D3
Bloemfontein 31 B4
Bloemhof 31 B4
Blois 8 C4
Bloomington 42 F4
Bloomsburg 42 E9
Blue Mts., Oreg., U.S.A. 40 A3
Blue Mts., Pa., U.S.A. 42 E9
Blue Nile → 29 E11
Blue Ridge Mts. 41 C10
Bluefield 42 G7
Bobcaygeon 42 C8
Bobo-Dioulasso 28 F4
Bóbr → 10 B8
Bobruysk 11 B15
Bochum 10 C4
Boden 6 E12
Bodø 6 E10
Bodrog → 11 D11
Bogor 22 D2
Bogotá 46 B2
Bogra 23 G12
Bohemian Forest = Böhmerwald 10 D7
Böhmerwald 10 D7
Bohol 22 C4
Bohol Sea 22 C4
Boise 40 B3
Bolgatanga 30 B1
Bolivia ■ 46 D3
Bolivian Plateau 46 D3
Bologna 12 B4
Bolshevik I. 18 B12
Bolton 7 E5
Bolzano 12 A4
Boma 32 F2
Bonifacio 8 F8
Bonn 10 C4
Boonville 42 F4
Boothia, Gulf of 39 A11
Boothia Pen. 38 A10
Borås 6 G10
Bordeaux 8 D3
Borisov 11 A15
Borneo 22 C3
Bornholm 6 G11
Bosnia-Herzegovina ■ 12 B7
Bosporus 13 D13
Boston 43 D12
Bothnia, G. of 6 F12
Botletle → 31 A3
Botoşani 11 E14
Botswana ■ 31 A3
Bouaké 28 G3
Bouar 32 C3
Boulogne-sur-Mer 8 A4
Bourbonnais 8 C5
Bourg-en-Bresse 8 C6
Bourges 8 C5
Bourgogne 8 C6
Bourke 34 G8
Bournemouth 7 F6
Bowling Green, Ky., U.S.A. 42 G4
Bowling Green, Ohio, U.S.A. 42 E6
Bracebridge 42 C8
Bräcke 6 F11
Bradford, U.K. 7 E6
Bradford, U.S.A. 42 E8
Braga 9 B1
Brahmanbaria 23 H13
Brahmani → 23 J11
Brahmaputra → 23 H12
Brăila 11 F14
Brampton 42 D8
Brandenburg 10 B7
Brandenburg □ 10 B6
Brandon 38 D10
Brandvlei 31 C3
Brantford 42 D7
Bras d'Or, L. 43 C17
Brasília 46 D5
Braşov 11 F13
Brassey Ra. 22 C3
Bratislava 11 D9
Brattleboro 43 D11
Brazil 42 F4
Brazil ■ 46 D5
Brazzaville 32 E3
Breda 10 C3
Bredasdorp 31 C3
Bregenz 10 E5
Breiðafjörður 6 B2
Bremen 10 B5
Bremerhaven 10 B5
Brenner P. 10 E6
Bréscia 12 B4
Brest, Belarus 11 B12
Brest, France 8 B1
Bretagne 8 B2
Brewer 43 C13
Breyten 31 B4
Briançon 8 D7
Bridgeport 43 E11
Bridgeton 43 F10
Bridgetown 44 P22
Bridgewater 43 C15
Brighton 7 F6
Bríndisi 13 D7
Brisbane 34 F9
Bristol 7 F5
Bristol Channel 7 F4
British Columbia □ 38 C7
British Isles 4 E5
Brits 31 B4
Britstown 31 C3
Brittany = Bretagne 8 B2
Brive-la-Gaillarde 8 D4
Brno 11 D9
Brocken 10 C6
Brockville 43 C10
Broken Hill 34 G7
Brooks Ra. 38 B5
Bruay-en-Artois 8 A5
Bruce, Mt. 34 E2
Brugge 10 C2
Brunei ■ 22 C3
Brunswick, Germany 10 B6
Brunswick, U.S.A. 43 D13
Brussels 10 C3
Bryan 42 E5
Bryansk 14 D5
Bucaramanga 46 B2
Bucharest 11 F14
Buckhannon 42 F7
Buckingham 43 C10
Bucyrus 42 E6
Budapest 11 E10
Buena Vista 42 G8
Buenos Aires 47 F4
Buffalo 42 D8
Bug → 11 B11
Buh → 15 E5
Bujumbura 32 E5
Bukavu 32 E5
Bukittinggi 22 D2
Bulandshahr 23 E6
Bulawayo 33 J5
Bulgaria ■ 13 C11
Bunbury 34 G2
Bundaberg 34 E9
Bundi 23 G5
Buraydah 24 C3
Burgas 13 C12
Burgersdorp 31 C4
Burgos 9 A4
Burgundy = Bourgogne 8 C6
Burkina Faso ■ 30 B1
Burlington, Vt., U.S.A. 43 C11
Burlington, Wis., U.S.A. 42 D3
Burlyu-Tyube 18 E9
Burma ■ 25 C8
Burnie 34 J8
Bursa 13 D13
Buru 22 D4
Burundi ■ 32 E5
Bushehr 24 C4
Butler 42 E8
Buton 22 D4
Butterworth 22 C2
Butuan 22 C4
Buzău 11 F14
Bydgoszcz 11 B9
Byelorussia = Belarus ■ 11 B14
Bytom 11 C10

Cabinda □ 32 F2
Cabonga, Réservoir 42 B9
Čačak 13 C9
Cáceres 9 C2
Cadillac 42 C5
Cádiz 9 D2
Caen 8 B3
Cagayan de Oro 22 C4
Cágliari 12 E3
Cahors 8 D4
Caicos Is. 45 C10
Cairns 34 D8
Cairo 29 B11
Calabar 30 D3
Calábria □ 12 E7
Calais, France 8 A4
Calais, U.S.A. 43 C14
Calamian Group 22 B3
Calapan 22 B4
Calcutta 23 H12
Caledon 31 C2
Caledon → 31 C4
Calgary 38 C8
Cali 46 B2
Calicut 25 D6
California □ 40 C2
California, G. of 44 B2
Calitzdorp 31 C3
Callao 46 D2
Caltanissetta 12 F6
Calvi 8 E8
Calvinia 31 C2
Camagüey 45 C9
Camargue 8 E6
Cambay, G. of 23 J4
Cambodia ■ 22 B2
Cambrai 8 A5
Cambrian Mts. 7 E5
Cambridge, U.K. 7 E7
Cambridge, Mass., U.S.A. 43 D12
Cambridge, Md., U.S.A. 43 F9
Cambridge, Ohio, U.S.A. 42 E7
Cambridge Bay 38 B9
Camden 43 F10
Cameroon ■ 30 C4
Cameroun, Mt. 30 D3
Campánia □ 12 D6
Campbellsville 42 G5
Campbellton 43 B14
Campeche 44 D6
Campeche, G. of 44 D6
Campina Grande 46 C6
Campinas 47 E5
Campo Grande 46 E4
Campos 46 E5
Camrose 38 C8
Can Tho 22 B2
Canada ■ 38 C10
Canadian Shield 39 C10
Canandaigua 42 D9
Canary Is. 28 C1
Canaveral, C. 41 E10
Canberra 34 H8
Cannes 8 E7
Canso 43 C17
Cantabria □ 9 A4
Cantabrian Mts. 9 A3
Canterbury 7 F7
Canton, N.Y., U.S.A. 43 C10
Canton, Ohio, U.S.A. 42 E7
Cap-Chat 43 A14
Cap-de-la-Madeleine 43 B11
Cape Breton I. 43 B17
Cape Charles 43 G10
Cape Coast 30 C1
Cape May 43 F10
Cape Town 31 C2
Cape Verde Is. ■ 27 E1
Cape York Peninsula 34 C7
Capreol 42 B7
Capri 12 D6
Caracas 46 A3
Carbondale 43 E10
Carcassonne 8 E5
Cardiff 7 F5
Caribbean Sea 45 E10
Caribou 43 B13
Carleton Place 43 C9
Carletonville 31 B4
Carlisle 42 E9
Carmaux 8 D5
Carmi 42 F3
Carnarvon, Australia 34 E1
Carnarvon, S. Africa 31 C3
Carnegie, L. 34 F3
Caro 42 D6
Carolina 31 B5
Caroline Is. 36 G6
Carpathians 11 D11
Carpentaria, G. of 34 C6
Carpentras 8 D6
Cartagena, Colombia 46 A2
Cartagena, Spain 9 D5
Casablanca 28 B3
Cascade Ra. 40 A2
Casper 40 B5
Caspian Sea 15 F9
Cass City 42 D6
Castellón de la Plana 9 C5
Castelsarrasin 8 E4
Castilla La Mancha □ 9 C4
Castilla y Leon □ 9 B3
Castres 8 E5
Castries 44 N21
Cataluña □ 9 B6
Catanduanes 22 B4
Catánia 12 F6
Catanzaro 12 E7
Catskill 43 D11
Catskill Mts. 43 D10
Caucasus Mountains 15 F7
Caxias do Sul 47 E4
Cayenne 46 B4
Cayuga L. 42 D9
Cedar Rapids 41 B8
Cegléd 11 E10
Celebes Sea 22 C4
Celina 42 E5
Central African Rep. ■ 32 C4
Central Makran Range 24 C5
Cephalonia = Kefallinía 13 E9
Ceram 22 D4
Ceram Sea 22 D4
Ceres 31 C2
Cerignola 12 D6
České Budějovice 10 D8
Ceuta 9 E3
Cévennes 8 D5
Chad ■ 29 E8
Chakradharpur 23 H10
Chaleur B. 43 B15
Chalisgaon 23 J5
Chalon-sur-Saône 8 C6
Châlons-en-Champagne 8 B6
Chamba 23 C6
Chambal → 23 F7
Chambersburg 42 F9
Chambéry 8 D6
Champagne 8 B6
Champaign 42 E3
Champlain, L. 43 C11
Chandigarh 23 D6
Chandpur 23 H13
Changchun 21 B7
Changde 21 D6
Changsha 21 D6
Changzhou 21 C6
Chanthaburi 22 B2
Chapleau 42 B6
Chapra 23 G10
Chardzhou 18 F8
Chārīkār 23 B2
Charleroi 10 C3
Charles, C. 43 G10
Charleston, Ill., U.S.A. 42 F3
Charleston, S.C., U.S.A. 41 D11
Charleston, W. Va., U.S.A. 42 F7
Charleville 34 F8
Charleville-Mézières 8 B6
Charlevoix 42 C5
Charlotte, Mich., U.S.A. 42 D5
Charlotte, N.C., U.S.A. 41 C10
Charlottesville 42 F8
Charlottetown 43 B16
Charolles 8 C6
Charters Towers 34 E8
Chartres 8 B4
Châteaubriant 8 C3
Châteaulin 8 B1
Châteauroux 8 C4
Châtellerault 8 C4
Chatham, N.B., Canada 43 B15
Chatham, Ont., Canada 42 D6
Chattanooga 41 C9
Chaumont 8 B6
Cheb 10 C7
Cheboksary 14 C8
Cheboygan 42 C5
Chechenia □ 15 F8
Chedabucto B. 43 C17
Chełm 11 C12
Chelyabinsk 18 D8
Chelyuskin, C. 18 B12
Chemnitz 10 C7
Chenab → 23 D3
Chengdu 20 C5
Cher → 8 C4
Cherbourg 8 B3
Cheremkhovo 18 D12
Cherepovets 14 C6
Cherkassy 15 E5
Chernigov 14 D5
Chernobyl 11 C16
Chernovtsy 11 D13
Cherski Ra. 18 C16
Chesapeake B. 42 F9
Chester 43 F10
Chesterfield Inlet 38 B10
Chesuncook L. 43 B13
Chhatarpur 23 G7
Chiai 21 D7
Chiba 19 B7
Chibougamau 43 A10
Chibougamau L. 43 A10
Chicago 42 E4
Chiclayo 46 C2
Chicopee 43 D11
Chicoutimi 43 A12
Chidley, C. 39 B13
Chieti 12 C6
Chihli, G. of 21 C6
Chihuahua 44 B3
Chile ■ 47 F2
Chilka L. 23 K10
Chillán 47 F2
Chillicothe 42 F6
Chilpancingo 44 D5
Chilton 42 C3
Chilung 21 D7
Chimborazo 46 C2
Chimbote 46 C2
Chimkent 18 E8
China ■ 21 C6
Chindwin → 25 C8
Chingola 33 G5
Chinon 8 C4
Chíos 13 E12
Chipata 33 G6
Chipman 43 B15
Chita 18 D13
Chitral 23 B3
Chittagong 23 H13
Cholet 8 C3
Chŏngjin 21 B7
Chongqing 20 D5
Chorzów 11 C10
Choybalsan 21 B6
Christchurch 35 J13
Christiana 31 B4
Chukot Ra. 18 C19
Chumphon 22 B1
Chur 10 E5
Churchill →, Man., Canada 38 C10
Churchill →, Nfld., Canada 39 C13
Churu 23 E5
Chushal 23 C7
Chuvashia □ 14 C8
Cicero 42 E4
Ciechanów 11 B11
Ciénaga 46 A2
Cienfuegos 45 C8
Cincinnati 42 F5
Cinto, Mte. 8 E8
Circleville 42 F6
Cirebon 22 D2
Citlaltépetl 44 D5
Ciudad Bolívar 46 B3
Ciudad Guayana 46 B3
Ciudad Juárez 44 A3
Ciudad Madero 44 C5
Ciudad Obregón 44 B3
Ciudad Real 9 C4
Ciudad Victoria 44 C5
Clanwilliam 31 C2
Claremont 43 D11
Clarksburg 42 F7
Clarksville 41 C9
Clearfield 42 E8
Clermont-Ferrand 8 D5
Cleveland 42 E7
Clifton Forge 42 G8
Cluj-Napoca 11 E12
Clyde → 7 D4
Coast Mts. 38 C7
Coast Ranges 40 B2
Coaticook 43 C12
Coatzacoalcos 44 D6
Cobourg 42 D8
Cochabamba 46 D3
Cochin 25 E6
Cochrane 42 A7
Cockburn I. 42 C6
Cod, C. 41 B13
Cognac 8 D3
Coimbatore 25 D6
Coimbra 9 B1
Colebrook 43 C12
Colesberg 31 C4
Colima 44 D4
Collingwood 42 C7
Colmar 8 B7
Cologne 10 C4
Colombia ■ 46 B2
Colombo 25 E6
Colón 44 H14
Colonial Heights 42 G9
Colorado □ 40 C5
Colorado →, N. Amer. 40 D4
Colorado →, U.S.A. 41 E7
Colorado Plateau 40 C4
Colorado Springs 40 C6
Columbia 41 D10
Columbia → 40 A2
Columbia, District of □ 42 F9
Columbus, Ga., U.S.A. 41 D10
Columbus, Ind., U.S.A. 42 F5
Columbus, Ohio, U.S.A. 42 F6
Comilla 23 H13
Communism Pk. 18 F9
Como 12 B3
Como, L. di 12 B3
Comodoro Rivadavia 47 G3
Comorin, C. 25 E6
Comoros ■ 27 H8
Compiègne 8 B5
Conakry 28 G2
Concepción 47 F2
Conchos → 44 B3
Concord 43 D12
Congo ■ 32 E3
Congo = Zaïre → 32 F2
Coniston 42 B7
Conneaut 42 E7
Connecticut □ 43 E11
Connecticut → 43 E11
Connellsville 42 E8
Connersville 42 F5
Constance, L. 10 E5
Constanţa 11 F15
Constantine 28 A6
Conway 43 D12
Cook, Mt. 35 J13
Cook Is. 35 E17
Cook Strait 35 J13
Copenhagen 6 G10
Copper Harbor 42 B4
Coppermine 38 B8
Coppermine → 38 B8
Coral Sea 36 J7
Corbin 42 G5
Córdoba, Argentina 47 F3
Córdoba, Spain 9 D3
Cordova 38 B5
Corfu 13 E8
Corinth, G. of 13 E10
Cork 7 F2
Corner Brook 39 D14
Corning 42 D9
Cornwall 43 C10
Coromandel Coast 25 D7
Coronation Gulf 38 B8
Corpus Christi 40 E7
Corrientes 47 E4
Corry 42 E8
Corse, C. 8 E8
Corsica 8 F8
Corte 8 E8
Cortland 43 D9
Cosenza 12 E7
Coshocton 42 E7
Costa Blanca 9 C5
Costa Brava 9 B7
Costa del Sol 9 D3
Costa Dorada 9 B6
Costa Rica ■ 45 F8
Côte d'Azur 8 E7
Côte-d'Ivoire = Ivory Coast ■ 28 G3
Cotentin 8 B3
Cotonou 30 C2
Cotopaxi 46 C2
Cotswold Hills 7 F5
Cottbus 10 C8
Coudersport 42 E8
Council Bluffs 41 B7
Coventry 7 E6
Covington 42 F5
Cox's Bazar 23 J13
Cradock 31 C4
Craiova 11 F12
Cranbrook 38 D8
Crawfordsville 42 E4
Cremona 12 B4
Crete 13 G11
Creuse → 8 C4
Crimea 15 E5
Crişul Alb → 11 E11
Crişul Negru → 11 E11
Croatia ■ 10 F9
Crocodile → 31 B5
Crystal Falls 42 B3
Cuba ■ 45 C9
Cubango → 33 H4
Cúcuta 46 B2
Cuenca, Ecuador 46 C2
Cuenca, Spain 9 B4
Cuernavaca 44 D5
Cuiabá 46 D4
Culiacán 44 C3
Culpeper 42 F9
Cumberland 42 F8
Cumberland Plateau 41 C10
Cúneo 12 B2
Curitiba 47 E5
Cuttack 23 J10
Cuxhaven 10 B5
Cuyahoga Falls 42 E7
Cuzco 46 D2
Cyclades 13 F11
Cynthiana 42 F5
Cyprus ■ 24 B2
Czech Rep. ■ 10 D8
Częstochowa 11 C10

Da Nang 22 B2
Dacca 23 H13
Dadra and Nagar Haveli □ 23 J4
Dadu 23 F1
Dagestan □ 15 F8
Dagupan 22 B4
Dahod 23 H5
Dakar 28 F1
Dakhla 28 D1
Dalhousie 43 A14
Dalian 21 C7
Dallas 41 D7
Dalmatia 12 C7
Daloa 28 G3
Damaraland 31 A2